BE THE BANK

HOW TO EARN HIGH RETURNS SECURELY BY LENDING TO SMEs

RICHARD ADMIRAAL

© 2014 RICHARD ADMIRAAL. ALL RIGHTS RESERVED

NO PART OF THIS WORK MAY BE REPRODUCED OR STORED IN AN INFORMATIONAL RETRIEVAL SYSTEM, WITHOUT THE EXPRESS PERMISSION OF THE PUBLISHER IN WRITING.

ISBN: 9781928155423

PUBLISHED BY:
10-10-10 PUBLISHING
MARKHAM, ON
CANADA

ACKNOWLEDGEMENTS

I wish to thank my colleagues at The Route – **Finance** who so freely shared their resources and expertise in the preparation of this book. It is my distinct pleasure to work so closely with all of you, authorities in your own right. Without your participation, this book could not have been written. I am also thankful to all the SME borrower executives who took their time to provide relevant and insightful feedback on accessing funding from The Route – **Finance**. It has been encouraging to read that the vast majority of the comments were positive, often complimentary. I am also grateful to The Route – **Finance** Members who have let me know their thoughts on all aspects of the Private Debt Platform proposition. The comments have been insightful and illuminating, and have helped to evolve and mould the offering and processes to help all stakeholders.

Richard Admiraal
October 2014

FOREWORD
by Bob Wigley

One of the repercussions of the credit crunch has been the negative impact on funding for small businesses. Increased capital requirements and smaller balance sheets for banks have denied credit for companies looking to expand in a growing economy.

The Route – **Finance**'s Private Debt Platform (PDP) aims to bring together private investors and Small to Medium-sized Enterprises (SMEs) by matching expanding companies with individuals looking for strong returns — returns not readily available in a low interest rate environment in which many asset classes appear overvalued.

The Route – **Finance**'s success has been in matching market professionals (often bankers themselves) who are prepared to offer collateralised loans to companies denied funding by overly conservative and capital-constrained banks. Individuals, risk averse by nature, have access to The Route – **Finance**'s due diligence, which aims to source borrowers with secure, realisable assets, while SMEs can access passive funds unencumbered by the sometimes stifling bank bureaucracy.

The Route – **Finance**'s PDP clearly provides not only an accessible source of capital, but can also play a vital role in facilitating the growth of SMEs. Systemic failure, such as that experienced by the global financial systems in 2008, is often solved by the ingenuity of individuals outside of the system. The Route – **Finance**'s success in the launch of its PDP is just one example where common sense, allied to sound business practice, can help repair funding streams while offering opportunity. This platform, bringing together as it does both parties under an umbrella of quantifiable risk, shows how borrowers and lenders can benefit from the inadequacy of the banking system and at the same time provides an object lesson in how economic recovery can be supported.

The Route – **Finance**'s Private Debt Platform certainly seems to be making a useful contribution to personal investors' access to a relatively low risk high return asset class whilst simultaneously providing much needed growth capital to SMEs.

Be the Bank

Bob Wigley was Chairman of Merrill Lynch, Europe, Middle East and Africa until 2009, as well as sitting on the Court of the Bank of England for the period leading up to and during the period of the financial crisis. Today he is Chairman of Tantalum Corporation plc, Stonehaven Search LLP, NetOTC, Captive Minds Communications Group Ltd, and Justinvesting Ltd and is an investor and entrepreneur. He is a Non Executive Director of the Qatar Financial Centre and Chairman of its Audit Committee. He is a member of the International Business Advisory Board of British Airways plc, sits on the Advisory Boards of the venture capital firm Bluegem Capital partners LLP and TheCityUk and is a Trustee of the Peter Jones Foundation. He is a member of the Advisory Boards of Cranfield School of Management's Doughty Centre for Corporate Social Responsibility, and Tetronics International Ltd, and is a Visiting Fellow of Oxford University and Chairman of Oxford University's Centre for Corporate Reputation. He chairs the Courtyard Appeal for the Royal College of Music and sits on its Council. He is a Fellow of the Institute of Chartered Accountants and has a business degree and an honorary doctorate from the University of Bath.

TABLE OF CONTENTS

Acknowledgements	i
Foreword	iii
Table of Contents	vii
Introduction	1
What Is An "SME"?	2
The Financing Problem For SMEs Has Reached Critical Levels	7
What Is A Cash Starved SME To Do?	13
Understanding Asset Based Financing	21
Becoming The Bank	22
Why The Route – **Finance** Can Work So Well For Investors	24
Case Study One	27
Show Me The Profit	31
Bonus #1: A comparison tool to show returns against other asset classes	32
How The Route – **Finance** Works for Small Businesses	33
Case Study Two	36
The Investment and Lending Process	39
Case Study Three	49

Case Study Four	61
Case Study Five	66
Bonus #2: A "Charge Free" assessment of your suitability to use "secured loans at unsecured lending rates"	69
Why The Route – **Finance** Works for Participants	70
There Is Always Demand For Secure Loans	70
Becoming The Bank	71
How To Become A Private Debt Platform Participant	72
How Does The Private Debt Platform Work?	74
Pensions and Self Invested Personal Pension (SIPP) Accounts	79
Who Can Have A SIPP?	83
Bonus #3: The key aspects to consider for using your pension to mandate capital to secure loans	86
Case Study Six	87
Commonly Asked Questions and Answers	93
Case Study Seven	103
Why Use The Route – **Finance**?	107
The Route – **Finance**'s Ten Defining Differences for Secured Loans on the Private Debt Platform	108

An Encouraging Postscript	110
Bonus #4: Complimentary The Route – **Finance** Membership	114
Appendix	115
Testimonials	116

INTRODUCTION

You may not have noticed, if you are not the head of a small- or medium-sized company, but the composition of the business sector in the United Kingdom has radically altered over the past two decades. Large corporations no longer constitute 'the large player' in the UK economy. Today, small and medium-sized enterprises (SMEs) predominate, accounting for over 99 % of all private sector businesses. Today, this "small business revolution" continues at an accelerated pace, with no indications of slowing down.

This growth in the commercial impact of SMEs has swept away many of the old methods and much of the "business as usual" traditional corporate culture, replacing it with a need for new ideas, innovations and methods of doing business. Perhaps nowhere is this more visible than when it comes to investing and the obtaining of debt finance. As business people and investors, our role is not only to understand this phenomenon but also to predict how it will evolve, and to capitalize on this distortion between:

- The low risk to capital an investor is asked to take on loans secured on realisable saleable assets; and
- The return that borrowers are prepared to pay for a source of guaranteed funding for suitable loans.

Introduction

Picking up this book is the first step to capitalizing on the small business revolution. Within these pages, you will find out how to boost the economy and your bank balance at the same time. "How?" you ask. By being the bank, of course.

What is an "SME"?

Before we get to the how, we should deal with the why. Although it is important to understand how to invest in small businesses, it is perhaps as important to understand why the need has arisen. For that, we have to start at the beginning, with a discussion of what a small- or medium-sized enterprise is and why traditional lending has failed that sector in the main. As with any investment, if you are going to invest in any SME, you probably should have a good understanding of what they are and what makes them tick.

That leads to the first question. What is an SME? It sounds as if it should be an easy question to answer, but it is not. The fundamental issue for clarifying what constitutes an SME is that there is no consistent definition — even within government literature. Authoritative organisations disagree on which criteria should be used. Some choose the number of employees and others financial parameters, specifically:

Companies House records for accounting requirements: Sections 382 and 465 of the Companies Act of 2006 define a small company as one that has annual turnover of not more than £6.5 m, a balance sheet of not more than £3.26 m and not more than 50 employees. A medium-sized company has a turnover of not more than £25.9 m, balance sheet of not more than £12.9 m and not more than 250 employees.

HM Revenue & Customs (HMRC) uses one overall definition of an SME, which is a business with not more than 500 employees and an annual turnover not exceeding £100 m. This is the qualifying definition for the purpose of Research and Development Tax Relief.

The Department for Business Innovation and Skills defines an SME as a business with less than 250 employees.

The European Union's definition is adopted by other branches of government, it states:
- Micro businesses — 0 to 9 employees
- Small businesses — 10 to 49 employees
- Medium businesses — 50 to 249 employees

For the purposes of investment, it does not really matter which yardstick you use, but for the purposes of this book we will use the European Union's definition, which is the most widely used.

Introduction

By focusing strictly on the number of employees, rather than on revenue generated, we shall be able to examine better the struggle facing SMEs in the UK. For owners of these businesses, having this distinction will make it easier to understand the size of the company that we are discussing (which is sometimes easier than talking about revenue or turnover). This will also allow us to examine how investors and SMEs can work together to bring about significant, mutual benefits.

SMEs Are Big Business In The United Kingdom

Do not let their size fool you. Regardless of the definition being used, it is unquestionable that SMEs comprise a critical sector of the UK economy. The SME sector is significantly growing each year. In fact, SMEs comprise the fastest growing sector of business in UK and are enormously important to the continued growth and well-being of the British economy overall.

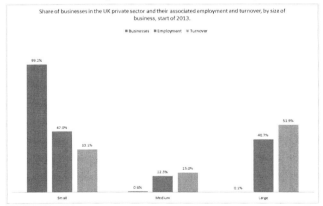

Source: BIS, Business population estimates, 2012, p 4

According to the Department for Business Innovation & Skills, as of 2010 there were a record number (a staggering 4.5 m) of private sector businesses in Britain. NatWest Business Sense reported that Companies House recorded 455,000 newly registered companies in the 2011/2012 financial year, up from 400,000 the year before.

This increase in company creation in the small business sector was emphatically praised by David Cameron in 2013 who said:

> "To get Britain on the rise we need a whole new economy, more enterprising, more aspirational ... and it is taking shape already. We're getting our entrepreneurial streak back: last year the rate of new business creation was faster than any other year in our history. Let me repeat that. The rate at which new businesses started – (was) faster than any year on record!"

According to the Federation of Small Business (FSB), the number of SMEs has risen to such heights that 99.9 % of all private sector businesses in the UK are considered to be SMEs. Also, according to a December 2012 report from Parliament, 96 % of all private sector businesses in the UK are micro businesses, employing less than ten people.

Introduction

Some of the other statistics from the FSB are similarly revealing; as of the beginning of 2013:
- SMEs accounted for 59.3 % of private sector employment and 48.1 % of private sector turnover.
- SMEs employed 14.4 m people.
- SMEs had a combined turnover of £1,600 bn.

In addition, for 2013:
- A record 526,446 new companies were registered in 2013 beating 484,224 for 2012.
- London was the top region with 152,084 — 29 % of the total.
- More than 25 % of these in London are in East London, which incorporates 'Tech City' technology businesses that have been promoted by Government initiatives.

UK SME Population Hits A Six-Year Post-Recession High

The number of active SMEs in UK reached a six-year high of 2.16 m in 2013, according to the SME Growth Monitor from the National Association for Commercial Finance Brokers (NACFB). The UK now has the most SMEs in business since before the downturn after two successive years of growth. Following the loss of 80,615 small businesses between 2008 and 2011, SME numbers have swelled by 4.2 % in the last two years (+86,435). Adam Tyler, CEO of the NACFB has commented:

"SMEs are the stalwarts of the economic recovery: they have played a vital role in brightening the UK's future prospects. By fuelling activity in greater numbers across the majority of UK industries, they have helped rebuild a strong foundation for further growth. This not only opens up more jobs but also boosts those larger employers who count SMEs in their supply chain or rely on the essential services they provide. 20.5 % of midsize SMEs (turnover of between £2.5 m & £100 m) are recording revenue growth of 33 % or higher over the last three years."

The Financing Problem for SMEs Has Reached Critical Levels

It would seem likely that, with this much influence on the marketplace, SME owners would not have problems obtaining the funding that they need to start and grow their businesses. However, you will not be surprised to learn (unless you have never watched or read business news in the last five years) that small businesses are facing a funding crisis. There is a mushrooming financial deficit for SMEs, and it shows no sign of abating.

There is no other single issue facing the sector today which has received more news coverage or which impedes the natural growth of SMEs more than their inability to obtain sufficient finance in a timely fashion. Banks will no longer lend sufficient

Introduction

money to SMEs, despite their protestations. Owners of SMEs have lost faith in the mainstream banking institutions and their processes, and have turned to other sources to obtain the funding that they need to both invest in their businesses and to maintain a healthy cash flow. Indeed a very common declaration from SME borrowers is that they will never approach a bank again — 'They take far too long, they are far too intrusive and then they invariably say no!'

Here are some disturbing figures for SMEs:
- In 2011, 60 % of SMEs were turned down by their banks for loans, overdrafts or overdraft extensions. That compares with only 4 % in 2007.
- The Bank of England published its assessment of the latest trends in lending (Bank of England Trends in Lending April 2012) to the UK economy. Key points from the report were:
  - Lending growth for all SMEs has been negative since late 2009.
  - Lending by UK banks and building societies to businesses decreased by around £ 9 bn in the three months prior to February 2012.
  - Net monthly flow of lending in February 2012 was at its lowest in almost two years.

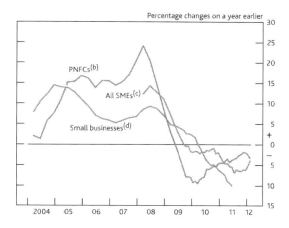

*Graph depicting lending to small and medium-sized businesses.
Source: Bank of England Trends in Lending report, April 2012.
Note: A PNFC is a Private Non-Financial Corporation.*

In a *Daily Telegraph* article published in the Business Section, 10th May 2012, it was reported, "British companies will have to find between £220 billion & £268 billion of new financing to fund their growth plans, as well as refinancing hundreds of billions of existing debt." This could create a so-called "perfect storm for credit markets".

Businesses are not alone. "The consequences of this are already being felt in the rising cost of borrowing from the largest banks to homebuyers," states the *Daily Telegraph*. The lack of funding across the board, and particularly the lack of funding available

Introduction

to businesses, has "led to a shrinkage in the amount of credit available to businesses and soaked up some of the investor demand for new debt".

The end result is that banks are lending less to SMEs and in turn SMEs are ceasing to approach banks for funding as their primary means of raising capital. As the regulations increase, it seems unlikely that SMEs will ever go back to traditional bank financing.

Significantly, SMEs are already no longer showing any particular interest in obtaining bank financing. Owners are put off by the lengthy and intrusive assessment process, especially as they have the perception they may very well be refused credit at the end. They are disinclined to pursue a process with so little likelihood of success. Simply, the process is misaligned with SMEs' need and timing for finance.

The amount of needed funding for SMEs, however, has not decreased. In fact, with so many new SMEs starting, the demand has increased, and shows no signs of slowing. Banks, however, simply will not loosen their lending purse strings for SMEs.

The confidence factor is also reflected in a November 2012 small business survey by Western Union, the global payment services business. Data from 600 small and medium-sized exporters showed 68 % were confident about the economic outlook, an increase of more than 12 % on the previous quarterly survey and the highest since the review started three years ago. Lending to corporates shrank an estimated 4 % last year, hitting the lowest level since 2006.

John Longworth, Director General of the British Chambers of Commerce, said "How do we turn good growth into really great, sustainable growth? In my mind, it is all about finding ways to boost business investment, so that small companies can grow to become medium-sized companies, and these businesses can then become the global wealth creators of the future."

Although official figures show that business investment increased by 1.4 % in the third quarter of 2013, it remains significantly (26 %) below its pre-crisis peak in 2008.

Xavier Rolet, Chief Executive of the London Stock Exchange Group, was quoted in *The Daily Telegraph*, 28th November 2013: "It is a pressing and ongoing issue. In the UK SMEs remain far too reliant on debt. More than 50 % of SMEs use credit card debt to fund their business. SMEs are the lifeblood of the UK economy – an army of 4.5 m companies".

Government adviser Lawrence Tomlinson accused banks of loading punitive charges on struggling companies to maximise

Introduction

returns and bonuses and of "making directors passengers in their own businesses." Mr. Tomlinson, who was brought in to the Business Department to represent entrepreneurs' interests, said he was struck by the "utter fear" companies have about speaking out against banks' behaviour because of threats over "their facility being removed, BACS facilities restrained, or being subject to civil or criminal action". He has also said that:

> "There's a huge disconnect between what banks are saying and what we are seeing. Businesses are being destroyed and people's lives are being ruined by really bad behaviour. Figures which show that four in five applications for loans are accepted by banks are "extremely misleading", he said, because so many businesses are being "actively deterred from accessing finance before being given the chance to apply."
>
> "There is a complete lack of trust towards the banks, and in many cases, this is ... justifiable. This is coupled by an astonishing fear of the banks, no one dares tell it as it is."

Only 30 % of small businesses planning to seek finance were confident their bank would say yes. If SMEs are the engine room for UK growth, what chance does the recovery stand if businesses don't believe banks will finance their growth plans? The performance of the Enterprise Finance Guarantee and the Funding for Lending schemes does not suggest banks are more prepared to lend to SMEs. According to BDRC Continental's recent SME *Finance Monitor* for the third quarter of 2013, SMEs remain sceptical about their chances of securing bank finance. Of the 15,000 small firms surveyed for the study, only 37 % of those planning to apply for finance believe their application would be approved.

Bank of England data showed on 3rd February 2014 what business groups described as proof that corporate funding channels were "damaged". Net lending to non-financial firms declined £1.9 bn in December, following November's sharp drop of £4.6 bn, which represented the biggest fall since records began in 2011. The data also showed net lending to SMEs fell £1.2 bn, after edging up £165 m in November.

The data also showed a widening disparity between interest rates offered to big corporations and small businesses.

What Is a Cash Starved SME To Do?

A recent survey of 5,000 small and medium-sized businesses revealed the number seeking finance has risen from 39 % to 44 %. The number of businesses looking to grow in the next 12 months has also risen to 51 % — the highest since the survey began.

Introduction

Although alternative methods of financing are growing, the six lending institutions — Santander, Barclays, HSBC, Lloyds, Nationwide and Royal Bank of Scotland — account for over 70 % of business lending.

In the face of these seemingly overwhelming obstacles, SMEs have been forced to search for credible alternative funding sources. Many have taken the obvious step of looking to themselves, either by reinvesting company profits or by approaching their own shareholders for money. Others have turned to family, friends, their own personal savings or even credit cards to bankroll their business ventures. These avenues alone cannot meet the demand. Thus, a large proportion has sought financing from private investors.

Many SMEs still struggle to secure the funding they need to expand, and the British Private Equity and Venture capital association (BVCA) said corporate venture capital was an "untapped and potentially huge source" of funding. According to the BVCA, 90 % of businesses that private equity and venture capital invest in are SMEs.

Businesses, particularly small and mid-sized companies, are in debt to their suppliers and customers and this is limiting cash flow and could damage the recovery. As *The Daily Telegraph* wrote on 1st June 2012: "... an unprecented trade credit gap has grown steadily wider, as businesses have been borrowing from each other in the absence of bank funding."

"At £327 bn, trade credit (the granting of credit by non-financial firms to their customers) is now 20 % larger than the size of bank credit and has risen to become the biggest single source of funding to UK businesses."

"The report, which studied 15 m limited company reports that were filed between 1998 and 2012, showed that 80 % of everyday business-to-business transactions are on credit terms and, without it, UK commerce would grind to a halt."

"While there were examples of bad practice in supplier treatment, the research shows that large firms are the net providers of trade credit to small companies, with SMEs receiving £50 bn more than they advance in trade credit."

"This research follows news last week that traditional lending to small business had fallen by 20 % over the last 12 months."

Companies that back small and medium-sized businesses should be offered tax breaks to encourage more investors to provide the "missing piece" of funding to SMEs, according to a leading industry body.

Introduction

The BVCA said reintroducing tax breaks such as the Corporate Venturing Scheme (CVS) would encourage more investment. CVS was set up in 2000 by the Labour government and offered relief against corporation tax of up to 20 % and against losses for companies that bought minority stakes in smaller, high-risk companies. However, the scheme was wound up in 2010 because it was judged to be underused. Over a 10-year period, £132 m was invested in almost 600 small companies.

The CBI has called on George Osborne to support small and medium businesses' access to finance. The business group wants to see the government introduce an incentive, such as capital gains tax relief, for holding individual equity holding for more than five years. It also wants to see the Seed Enterprise Investment Scheme (SEIS) made permanent.

CBI Director-General John Cridland said equity finance had an important role to play but that the UK lags behind other EU countries in this area: "Many smaller firms say they would be more likely to use equity finance if the investment was longer-term, which is why we want a tax incentive to encourage this."

We can see in Europe the muddle where capital markets have not advanced in the same way as they have in the US, where 80 % of the lending to corporates in the US is done through the capital markets. It is not done through bank balance sheets which have deleveraged, and they are still able to be out there doing business.

"In Europe, over 80 % of the lending to corporates is done through banks, it is on the balance sheet, they haven't been able to deleverage and now they can't do lending," so said Bob Diamond, former CEO of Barclays Capital, in February 2014.

The Bank of England's attempt to promote small business lending by recalibrating the Funding for Lending Scheme (FLS) has failed to engineer an increase in lending to firms.

Figures released by the Bank showed that net lending to small and medium-sized businesses fell by £723 m in the first quarter of the year 2014, the first period in which the FLS applied solely to business loans.

The scheme was launched by the BoE and the Treasury in 2012. It aims to incentivise banks to lend by providing them with cheap credit, and originally applied to both mortgages and business lending.

Only a third of Britain's small businesses have turned to their banks for financing in the past quarter, the lowest level on record, according to the latest data.

Introduction

"Despite the Government's repeated efforts to boost bank lending for firms, the latest SME Finance Monitor found that 33 % of small firms reported using external finance, which includes bank loans, overdrafts and credit cards in the first quarter."

The Telegraph goes on to write in an article on 29th May: "At present the largest four banks account for over 80 % of UK SMEs' main banking relationships."

"The recent Department of Business, Innovation and Skills (BIS)/BMG Research study estimated that the majority (71 %) of businesses who seek funding only approach one provider. The study also noted that in more than half of all cases, the provider the SME approaches will be their main bank."

"The BIS/BMG Research study also found that 37 % of businesses appear to give up their search for finance and cancel their spending plans after their first rejection."

"The BIS/BMG Research study found that only 6 % of SMEs declined for loans are referred to alternative funding by their bank, and just a further 11 % are offered alternative funding or advice."

SMEs need to find approachable, informed investors to fund their companies and investors, as always, will seek investments that have acceptable risk for the likely return, whatever the size of the company. Of course, SMEs have always been higher risk investments than mid cap or blue chip, as they are more likely to fail, losing the investors their capital. The Route – **Finance** sources secured loans only where saleable, realisable assets can be pledged as security. Deciding where and when to invest is always a difficult decision for those who seek returns from the stock market.

This is why SMEs need to make themselves as attractive as possible to the broadest range of potential investors. How does a company make itself more attractive? How does an investor know whether certain SMEs are the right ones to lend money to? It can be a daunting task.

That is why I have written this book. *'Be the Bank'* will assist SMEs with assets, whether company or personal, to secure finance. It will also allow investors to achieve high returns without the risk normally inherent in that level of profit. It will teach you to separate the 'wheat from the chaff', both as an investor in avoiding inappropriate borrowers and as a company in not borrowing from the wrong lenders. Also in the case of the SME owner, how to show you are the wheat rather than the chaff.

Introduction

This book will explain in detail the process by which SMEs with assets can find qualified investors. Conversely, the book will also explain to the investor how to obtain high returns securely by lending to SMEs with assets, how to assess if the SME that you have found is right for you, and thus, whether you are ready to be the bank.

Chapter One
UNDERSTANDING ASSET BASED FINANCING

You may be thinking, "Certainly low risk/ high return investments sound perfect to me, but what is asset based financing?" The answer is simple, really. It is lending where the collateral for the loan is an asset or assets which are valued above the value of the loan capital plus interest; that is, these assets can be sold to repay the loan if, for any reason, the loan cannot be repaid and goes into default and the lenders elect to foreclose. Thus, different from the normal security that an investor has when lending to a company, i.e. the business staying in business and producing profits, the security is provided by tangible, realisable assets that can:

- Be easily valued;
- Find a ready marketplace; and
- Be sold easily.

Which would you rather have as security for your capital?
- The business plan of XYZ Ltd SME; or
- The business plan, plus XYZ's UK land and/or property, valued at in excess of 150 % of the loan capital plus interest.

Why is this important to an investor (other than for the obvious reason that they want to have as low a risk as possible)? It is because it allows you to have an attractively high return without the normal significant risk of capital loss.

It is really a win-win situation for the investor, as long as certain simple conditions are met. If the company pays back its loan, the investors get their loaned capital back plus the accrued interest. If the company fails to pay back the loan on time, and an extension cannot be agreed upon, the securitised assets are taken and sold to repay the investors. Minimal capital risk is involved.

Becoming the Bank

You can exploit the opportunity that has been created by the lack of bank lending to SMEs, to achieve high investment returns securely. This is where you, as an investor, have an opportunity to become the bank — to provide what SMEs need. Private investors, both in the UK and internationally, are recognising the potential in financing SMEs, and they are looking for ways to invest in this burgeoning market, whilst limiting the risk through proper sourcing and expert assessment of both the borrower and the loan.

However, many investors, even seeing the potential for high returns, are wary of investing in SMEs. They have questions that need answering. There is a lot of often specialised due diligence to be completed. It is a lot of work to find the right investment opportunities.

Private investment in SMEs is frightening for many investors and, to be fair, they have some legitimate concerns. Where do you find the right SMEs in which to invest? How do you make an accurate assessment of an SME's worthiness? How do you evaluate the collateral? In short, how do you decide which SMEs meet the requirement for obtaining high returns securely?

Certainly, with enough research, time and effort you can source the right debt investments. However:

- Do you have the time required to complete the assessment and due diligence?
- If you do, do you also have the comprehensive and specific knowledge to do so?
- If you do, can you also confirm you have the inclination to apply yourself to the task, rather than using that time and mental energy elsewhere?

Most investors are busy people with many demands on their time.

Why The Route – Finance Can Work so Well for Investors

What are investors looking for? The obvious answer is a short-term, very low risk, high return investment that they can understand and follow during its lifetime. Although, arguably, there are no 'nil-risk' investments, there are investments that can make a very strong case for being considered so.

In other words, there are investments that are low risk and still offer attractive returns. An investor needs to look for investments that offer such a distortion, in the investor's favour, between the returns offered and the perceived risk. The investments that do this the best are asset based debt investments. This type of investment can be categorised as a Secure High Return investment. There is of course constant demand for these loans where the investor can access 'secure loans at unsecured lending rates'.

That is why using a specialist company to source the investments is imperative. For example, using The Route – **Finance**'s specific vetting process, for SME investments eliminates most of the risk so that The Route – **Finance** can offer Secure High Return debt investments to its investors. It is easy to see why this combination can be considered as a win-win investment opportunity for its investors.

When The Route – **Finance** offers investments to its investor group, it is interested in providing investments in SMEs that have a probable and defined exit strategy, combined with realisable, saleable assets of far greater value than the loan capital plus interest. This is important, if those assets need to be sold on foreclosure. This allows the investor to obtain a targeted 15 % per annum for short-term loans.

What The Route – **Finance** is trying to do is meet the demand from SME companies which arguably the banks should be lending to and aren't! This is achieved by providing financing to SMEs with traditional banking-style underwriting, but without the post-2008 banking's lengthy, intrusive and often misleading process —the dreaded head office 'credit committee'.

That is where The Route – **Finance** can be an invaluable tool for an investor. By providing asset-based, secured financing opportunities to investors on its Private Debt Platform it does all the time-consuming and specialist work and the investors can mandate money with confidence and reap the rewards.

*"From an operational perspective, I believe that The Route – **Finance**'s Private Debt Platform has an efficient and effective process for bringing its secured loans to the Private Debt Platform Members. The procedure, from finding and assessing the loans, all the way through to informing Members is both challenging and varied. Each loan is different but the*

way in which the assessment process is conducted and then delivered to the Member investors, is the same. In the due diligence assessment, all aspects of the borrowing company, and the steps right through to when the funds are drawn down by the borrower, The Route – **Finance** *aims to complete in a way that is thorough but also hassle-free for the participants."*

Kyleigh Lynch
Senior Business Manager

CASE STUDY ONE

The Opportunity
The Route – **Finance** was approached by a themed restaurant/club/bar, with its flagship site in central London. The loan was for £1 m over a term of 24 months.

The Security
The security for the loan was the lease of the flagship site that had been independently valued at £1.1 m by a leading firm of surveyors. The lease had twelve years to run but, as it was a lease rather than a freehold interest, it was a depreciating asset.

The Pricing
- The loan would attract an interest premium for the Private Debt Platform (PDP) participants of 16 % per annum.
- In the event of non-repayment of the loan when it fell due, in either full or in part, a penalty premium of 2.5 % per month was to apply to the unpaid balance.

The Repayment
- The loan was due to be repaid with trading revenues.

Commentary
- The proposed loan was to be used to redevelop the London site as well as to provide part of the funding for the expansion of the business in China. The borrower had already raised some equity to fund most of the expansion and had secured a unit in an upmarket shopping mall in Shanghai. This site was expected to perform well once it had opened, six to twelve months into the loan term.
- Whilst there was tangible security available, it was not sufficient to cover the capital and interest in the event of foreclosure and sale of the security. In addition, the proposed exit for the loan was via trading revenues. This was very dependent on the successful delivery of the business plan.

The Key Risks
- The security available was not sufficient to cover the capital and interest.
- After a review of the proposal and business plan The Route – **Finance** was not confident that the borrower would be in a position to set aside the required money each month to repay the loan on time.

Assessment

- No security was available on any other assets, including any of the Chinese assets. The Route – **Finance** did consider offering the borrower a reduced loan amount of £750 k as an alternative, with the proviso that interest was to be repaid monthly rather than at the end of the term.
- The Route – **Finance** was not satisfied that the trading revenues would be sufficient to repay the loan on time and the application was declined.

LOAN DECLINED
And Not Presented to The Route – Finance's PDP Members

Guarantees are few and far between in the investment world, and you should always remember to read the small print! The Route – **Finance** believes the risk of capital loss in the secured loans it presents to its PDP Members is minimal. Once you have read about the detailed process in the next chapter, you will see that The Route – **Finance** is thorough and diligent in the sourcing and assessment of these secured loans.

We take care of all the details. In fact, The Route – **Finance** will do everything in the process except provide the loan capital. The Route – **Finance** will:

- Source the loans;
- Complete an objective assessment of the borrower and loan required;
- Negotiate the terms of the loan;
- Complete comprehensive 'due diligence' on each loan application;
- Instruct the lawyers who construct the legal paperwork;
- Complete the capital raise including providing concise details of the loan to the PDP participants;
- Act as Security Trustee to oversee and protect the PDP Members' interests, liaise with the borrower on the Members' behalf generally, and ensure adherence to the loan conditions as necessary. These duties will specifically include during the life of the loan:

- — Providing quarterly updates written by the borrower to the PDP Members;
  - — Dealing with any ad hoc advice or developments; and
  - — Liaising with the borrower and lawyers to repay the loan at the end of the term.
- Source new secured loans into which the loan capital plus interest can be reinvested;
- Deal with any end of loan variations that may arise if the borrower requires flexibility from the lenders because it is unable to repay the loan capital plus interest in full and on time. (NB: Any variation to the term can be implemented only with the agreement of the investors who can insist on immediate repayment if they choose and subsequent foreclosure if that is not complied with.)

Show Me the Profit

Of course, it all comes down in the end to making a profit. One of the attractive features of working with Secure High Return Investments is that you should be as certain, as anyone can be, of making a profit via the planned exit, an agreed variation or a foreclosure and sale of the assets. You are able to do so with a much higher return than you would normally receive from investments with comparable risk.

Understanding Asset Based Financing

Typically, secured loans sourced by The Route – **Finance** target an annual return of 15 %, although this may vary a little above or below that figure. This is for loan terms that rarely stretch beyond eighteen months. Considering that interest rate is for a loan secured on saleable, realisable assets, worth far more than the money lent, it is a very attractive way to make money with little risk to capital, whilst also providing the money to enable SMEs to deliver their business plans and grow.

Bonus #1:

Do you want an easy to use interactive tool that can easily show you what return, and thus how much money, you can expect from investing in Secured Loans via The Route – **Finance**'s Private Debt Platform, over difference timescales? It will also show you a comparison of this potential return against other asset classes, such as cash, property or equities. To gain access to this illuminating comparison tool, just go to *http://www.theroute-finance.com/be-the-bank* where the information and unrestricted access is provided without charge.

Chapter Two
HOW THE ROUTE – FINANCE WORKS FOR SMALL BUSINESSES

One of the reasons that private financing generally works best for SMEs is now probably obvious to you. As discussed earlier, obtaining finance from a traditional bank is nigh on impossible for many SMEs. Thus, the private sector is not only the best option it may very well be the only avenue available for obtaining a loan.

Going to the private market rather than a mainstream bank should not mean the vetting measures are any less stringent. Organisations such as The Route – **Finance** have to be very careful that they are introducing their clients to appropriate loans and borrowers.

One factor that ensures working through private financing is far superior to going to a bank is the process itself. It is a more personal and less intrusive process. Although private financing vetting requirements, at least through The Route – **Finance**, are very thorough, it is a very different experience from trying to borrow from a traditional bank. One of the most important differences is that the communication has a human touch, a human face if you will; an interaction with the people who actually make the decision to lend or not.

At The Route – **Finance** each borrower has a dedicated contact. If there is a question, an issue or a problem, they can talk directly to their contact rather than to a bank relationship manager who merely passes the message to and from the decision makers at the dreaded credit committee. Borrowers can pick up the phone and talk directly to their contact. Furthermore, The Route – **Finance** contact and the borrower can usually work through any issues logically and promptly. It is not about the loan fitting within an inflexible bank-lending matrix. It can be about the explanation behind the key financial information. It also has a great deal to do with the people to whom the money is being lent.

Lending approval through private investment firms like The Route – **Finance** is centered on a specific set of criteria. If there is a problem, and a solution cannot be found, it is not because the desire to solve it is not there, or that we do not wish to present the loan to the PDP Members. It is because the loan cannot satisfy the due diligence criteria and thus cannot be passed for presentation.

The Route – **Finance** is able to make a decision promptly. When working with The Route – **Finance**, a borrower is likely to receive:

- An initial assessment as to whether the loan is acceptable, subject to due diligence, within a few days;
- The completion of the due diligence within four weeks typically;
- The 'raise' of the money applied for normally a couple of weeks after that; and
- Completion of the legal paperwork and the release of the money within another couple of weeks.

The most important of these timeline issues is the initial assessment. The Route – **Finance** is able to let a borrower know within a few days if its loan, in principle, is suitable or not, subject to due diligence. This allows the SME's directors to know promptly whether they need to go elsewhere for their money.

CASE STUDY TWO

The Opportunity
The Route – **Finance** was approached by a renewable energy company based in Wales. The borrower required a loan of £3 m for 12 to 15 months.

The Security
The security for the loan was a twenty-acre site in Wales, valued at £7 m, that had planning permission to build an 'Energy from Waste' (EfW) facility.

The Pricing
- The loan was to attract an interest premium for the PDP participants of 17 % per annum.
- In the event of non-repayment of the loan when it fell due, in either full or in part, a penalty premium of 3 % per month was to apply to the unpaid balance.

The Repayment
- The £3 m was to be used to finance the completion of a business plan to build the EfW site. On completion of the business plan, an international mainstream bank was to

provide £183 m of project finance to both build the site and to repay the loan.

Commentary
- The site has been independently valued by a leading firm of surveyors at £7 m.
- The Route – **Finance** requested that the signed term sheets from the bank be provided as a 'condition precedent' of acceptance. Whilst these signed term sheets do not legally bind the bank to provide funds to the borrower, they are a significant indication that the bank intends to do so, assuming its terms can be satisfied.
- Of course, if the bank does not ultimately provide the funds, the site could be sold or another funding partner sought. There was a competitive tender process for the project finance and the bank that provided the signed terms had been successful in its proposal. It stood to make a healthy profit if the project succeeded.

The Key Risks
- The site valued at £7 m falling in value to below the loan capital plus interest amount; and
- The bank deciding not to finance the project.

Assessment
- The Route – **Finance** was confident that there was

*How The Route – **Finance** Works for Small Businesses*

sufficient security for the loan and, also, the valuation was supported by the surveyor's Professional Indemnity insurance cover. In addition, the exit for the loan was clearly defined with the bank's project finance of £183 m being pledged.
- The Route – **Finance** was satisfied with the security and the exit.

LOAN ACCEPTED
and presented to The Route – Finance's PDP Members*

* The loan was oversubscribed and the loan capital and interest are due to be repaid in full in January 2015.

The Investment and Lending Process

Locating Qualifying Secured Loans and Borrowers

Finding borrowers with appropriate secured loans is the first step in any lending process. It is also the most important step. Separating the wheat from the chaff — i.e. those who are suitable businesses to lend to, have business plans to provide strong exits and realisable, saleable assets in sufficient quantity, from those who do not — is crucial in providing the best secured loans for investors.

The way the process works is that potential borrowers contact The Route – **Finance** when they need funding and that they think will fit The Route – **Finance**'s requirements. This process applies to borrowers that we have worked with before or those who are introduced to The Route – **Finance** by previous borrowers.

Also, as we have been providing debt finance for over five years, The Route – **Finance**'s reputation often encourages potential borrowers to make direct contact. Other companies seeking financing, which have not done business with, or heard of, The Route – **Finance** before may be introduced by their own professional advisers.

*How The Route – **Finance** Works for Small Businesses*

The Route – **Finance** is also approached for funding by professional intermediaries or introducers who are aware of both The Route – **Finance**'s requirements and the borrower's needs and, for a fee, will make an introduction.

Initially, The Route – **Finance** assesses the loan application in terms of the key criteria, as listed below:
- The amount of money required;
- The term of the loan;
- The interest offered;
- The exit strategy (i.e. how the borrower intends to repay the loan capital plus interest);
- The assets being offered as security;
- What the company does; and
- The background to the business.

The most important aspect for the borrower is to provide complete and accurate information on both the security and the exit for the loan. These are the two key components for the initial assessment. If they are not satisfactory, the loan application will not proceed.

Assets Being Pledged as Security

In order for The Route – **Finance** to agree to offer the loan to its PDP investors for their participation there must be sufficient security of the right quality. Investors are looking for realisable assets that can be sold easily, if necessary.

Land and property are ideal assets as pledged security. Firstly, they are physical assets that are not moveable. Secondly, they can be readily valued by a professional surveyor. Thirdly, and most importantly, land and property can normally always be sold. This fact is the key for proposing an asset for use as security. It is not what value the asset has on the company's balance sheet that is relevant, but what it can be sold for, if the borrower defaults on repaying the loan and the sale proceeds need to repay the loan. The valuation is normally done on a '180 day' basis, i.e. what the asset could be sold for within six months.

The second item that investors are looking for is a realistic and probable exit for the loan and, preferably, a credible fallback alternative. The loans should be repaid in full and on time by the end of the loan term. On assessing the loan application, this point must be satisfied.

The proposed exit is therefore also key. In order to be accepted, and have investor interest, there has to be a credible exit by the end of the loan term. Typically, what The Route – **Finance** and its investors look for is a capital event that is likely to occur before the repayment date.

For example, a secured loan that The Route – **Finance** recently completed involved a block of apartments that was about to be built. Half of these had already been pre-sold, off-plan, with a 10 % non-refundable deposit. These sales served as the exit for the loan i.e. the sale proceeds of the apartment units once built and sold. The loan was for £1.5 m and the anticipated sale proceeds were £8.7 m.

Having checked that the borrower is *bona fide*, i.e. one you would want to lend money to, all other things being satisfactory, the two loan conditions that must be satisfied are the *security* and *exit*. Of course, other criteria are also important, but these are the most important ones. They have to be satisfied for The Route – **Finance** to consider assessing the proposal and are therefore not negotiable.

There is an internal checklist, including all the terms mentioned above, which covers all the relevant points — term, security, exit, premium and updates. Assuming all of these are satisfactory the project can proceed to due diligence. If any of the criteria are not satisfied, The Route – **Finance** advises the SME's directors accordingly, and they have to consider whether they can improve the proposal to meet the initial assessment requirements. Generally, the items that the borrower can consider are:

- Improving either the quantity and/or quality of the security; and/or
- Improving the exit relative to the amount borrowed; and/or
- Applying to borrow a smaller amount.

The Route – **Finance** is normally not interested in the borrower offering a higher interest rate. The security and the exit of the Secured loan are of paramount importance. If these items cannot be improved in order to satisfy the initial assessment, the loan application is declined.

Usually, once provided with the key information an initial assessment can be made and a project can then be either accepted (and it will proceed to signed terms and DD) or declined (if a satisfactory proposal cannot be made). The borrower (and where applicable the introducer) can then be told why the application will not be considered in its current format. The borrower can submit a revised proposal at a later date. The Route – **Finance** will reconsider it if it has been sufficiently adapted so as to fit within the requirements for an acceptable secured loan.

Due Diligence

All companies conduct DD slightly differently, but the process that The Route – **Finance** follows is to satisfy itself that it is both appropriate to lend to a particular borrower and that the proposed terms are appropriate for the PDP participants. The DD may throw up items that mean that The Route – **Finance**:

- Will not lend to this borrower; and/or
- Will not lend on the proposed terms

*(This illustrates that, unlike a traditional bank which generally either approves or denies a loan, The Route – **Finance** will work with a potential borrower, if the originally proposed terms are not acceptable, to determine if an appropriate revised proposal is attainable. The Route – **Finance** will give borrowers appropriate opportunity to make an improved offer one before the application is finally turned down).*

If a loan application passes the initial assessment, The Route – **Finance** can proceed to completing the DD necessary and being able to offer it to PDP Members. An email is sent to the borrower and, if there is one, the introducer, to let them both know that the initial assessment has been positive. The borrower is then asked to both sign an agreement, called a Term Sheet, and to pay the agreed DD fee.

The Term Sheet is confirmation of the loan terms that the borrower will present to the PDP Members assuming DD is completed successfully. It also includes the fee agreement between The Route – **Finance** and the borrower. It is signed both by the borrower and The Route – **Finance**. It is also signed by the introducer if one is involved.

The DD fee is 'Non-contingent' and is normally a percentage of the loan and forms part of the fee that The Route – **Finance** charges the borrower. 'Non-contingent' means that if the loan application does not pass the DD assessment, for any reason, the fee is not be refunded. It covers The Route – **Finance**'s time to complete the DD work and has two advantages for the PDP Member participants and The Route – **Finance**:

1. It ensures that the borrower provides accurate information in the initial assessment. There is no point in the borrower making untrue statements, exaggerating the positivity of its situation or omitting a negative as the DD will inevitably reveal the true situation and the loan application would consequently be declined.
2. It aligns the interests of The Route – **Finance** and its PDP participants. If the loan passes DD that is all very well and good, but if it fails there is no reason for The Route – **Finance** to seek to find a way for the application to pass just to ensure payment for work up to that point.

You might wonder, "Is that really necessary? Does that actually happen? Do people really provide inaccurate or misleading information or fail to disclose a negative item in order to try to obtain a loan?" The answer is most certainly, yes! In fact, it happens more often than you would think.

Most lenders have experienced this and The Route – **Finance** is no exception. A recent potential borrower made a loan application and stated that the security was worth £1m. It transpired in the DD that the security was worth $1/1000^{th}$ of that, £1,000. The loan application was rejected as the potential borrower was not able to provide adequate replacement security. In addition, as a consequence, the borrower was viewed as not a *bona fide* company to which to lend. This would affect any future applications for finance from the same company or directors.

The DD process is comprehensive. Typically, four weeks is required to produce the report although, in effect, the timescale is as long as it takes to receive a response from the slowest respondent. The Route – **Finance**'s reports are completed in-house and the financial information is reviewed by a chartered accountant. When external assessment is required, this expertise is contracted to provide an opinion. Once the report has been completed, and the loan application has achieved a pass, the report proceeds to The Route – **Finance**'s 'Sign off' process.

'Sign off' is an internal stage of The Route – **Finance**'s assessment process that ensures the necessary people review the DD report and confirm that a loan application that has passed

DD has been properly assessed. The report is reviewed by:

- **Iain Burke**: Head of The Route – **Finance**;

- **Simon Pimblett**: Head of The Route – **City wealth club**'s 'Research and Development' function;

- **Alan Gunner**: A chartered accountant who performs the Financial Director's role at The Route – **City wealth club**;

- **Richard Admiraal**: Director of The Route – **City wealth club** and the Senior Relationship Manager for PDP participants; and

- **Lisa McLeod**: Director of Operations at The Route – **City wealth club**.

In terms of the DD, once the loan application has been agreed to, offered to PDP participants and the raise of funds completed, an additional layer of DD is performed by The Route – **Finance**'s legal partners, currently EMW Law LLP. Importantly, although it is the borrower who pays the legal bills, EMW is instructed by The Route – **Finance** and not by the borrower. EMW ensures that the legal paperwork properly reflects the agreed loan terms. If it identifies anything that is not acceptable, the terms can be altered, or in extreme cases the application declined, right up until the legal paperwork is due to be signed by the PDP Member investors and the loan capital provided to the borrower.

CASE STUDY THREE

The Opportunity
The Route – **Finance** was approached by a company that was providing a data tracking service to the first division of a major European country's football league. The borrower applied for a loan of £750,000 for a term of twelve months.

The Security
The security for the loan was to be the money generated from a three-year contract with the league worth £1 m annually. The earnings were to be placed in a secured account to which the borrower was not allowed access.

The Pricing
- The loan was to attract an interest premium for the PDP participants of 15 % per annum.
- In the event of non-repayment of the loan when it fell due, either in full or in part, a penalty premium of 2 % per month was to apply to the unpaid balance.

The Repayment
- The loan was due to be repaid from the £1 m annual contract fee.

*How The Route – **Finance** Works for Small Businesses*

Commentary
- The £750,000 was to be used to satisfy the contract granted to the data tracking company by the football league. To satisfy the contract, the borrower was required to attend every league match and record relevant data for each game. Therefore, the borrower needed to purchase a fleet of vehicles and computer/server equipment.
- The data, number of passes, possession percentages, etc., would then be collected and made available for use by television broadcasters, gambling companies and the teams playing in that league.
- Although the contract for £1 m provided security for the loan, it was not considered sufficient as the £1 m was paid monthly in equal instalments throughout the ten month football season. It was agreed that an additional £1 m of assets would be added as further security. This comprised the existing equipment owned by the company, and the assets to be purchased with the loan money.

The Key Risks
- The football league going out of business within the loan term and not paying the £1 m annual contract fee.
- The borrower being unable to satisfy the contract with the league.

- The £1 m of equipment loses much of its value within the loan term.

Assessment
- As the football league was considered to be a strong counterparty, it was deemed unlikely that it would go out of business.
- It was also deemed unlikely that the borrower would not fulfill its contract as it had all the required funds, knowledge and equipment to deliver the contract.
- Whilst all of the equipment would depreciate, it was considered unlikely that it would lose sufficient value within the twelve-month term as to be worth less than the loan capital plus interest.
- The Route – **Finance** was satisfied with the security and exit.

LOAN ACCEPTED (with amendments) and presented to The Route – Finance's Platform Members*

* The loan was fully subscribed
and has now been repaid in full.

The Due Diligence Report Checklist

The DD is completed by the following of a detailed checklist. The Route – **Finance**'s process comprises three areas: 'Information', 'Evidence' and 'Questions':

Information

This part of the checklist is also divided into three sections and provides a synopsis of the project. Essentially, it is meant to ascertain as much information on the borrower as possible. The Route – **Finance** will always want to know:

1) Who the borrower company is;
2) Who the directors, shareholders and key management team are;
3) The company's registered and trading addresses;
4) How the funds are to be used by the borrower;
5) How much the borrower wishes to raise in total;
6) The participation allocation if The Route – **Finance** is only to provide part of the loan capital;
7) The loan term;
8) The proposed return;
9) The exit for the loan (How the loan capital and interest will be repaid); and
10) Who the borrower's professional advisers are: accountants, solicitors and bankers.

Evidence

This is the area of the checklist where The Route – **Finance** conducts research to validate all the information provided by the borrower. For example, the borrower may state that an asset has a particular value. The Route – **Finance** requires a recent valuation provided by an industry recognised valuer who is preferably a member of a professional body. The valuation is normally expected to be underwritten by the valuer's Professional Indemnity insurance so that on foreclosure, and sale of the assets, if the sale proceeds do not meet the valuation provided, the insurance policy can be claimed upon.

Questions

These are the questions posed by either The Route – **Finance** assessor who conducts the DD or the individuals, previously listed, who 'Sign off' the secured loan application. Upon reviewing the information provided, or the evidence gathered, there may be questions in order to completely understand, or to expand on the understanding of, the proposed loan, the loan application or the borrower company itself.

Here are some examples of the type of the questions that The Route – **Finance** has asked of borrowers:

- Have you approached a bank for this funding?
- If so what was the answer?
- Where else have you applied, or are you applying, for finance?
- Can you confirm that you can grant an exclusive first charge over the assets proposed as security?
- What is the intended exit for the loan?
- What happens if the intended exit does not occur?
- Why are you confident that the exit will occur?

Of course, there will also be individual questions that can only be determined by the nature of the loan itself.

Other parts of the checklist:

The Route – **Finance** calculates an in-house credit score for the borrower and its loan application. It is not a formal, bank style, credit score but serves the same purpose. It is generated by a computer program that was designed by The Route – **Finance**. The program asks a set of questions about the loan. Answers provided by the borrower, or yielded by the DD, are fed into the program, which then calculates a score — a rating for the loan — which is reviewed to see if the loan passes or fails in its current format. The credit score also allows the loan to be compared to other secured loan applications, or indeed any other investment.

For example, the program will ask questions such as "What is the interest being offered?" "Is there a currency risk?" and "In which country is the borrower and its assets based?" The score features as a percentage, with the pass mark being 65 %. The highest mark ever achieved was 71 %, the lowest 55 %. Of course, there are applications that would have achieved lower marks than this but they will already have been eliminated by the initial assessment.

The in-house credit review score gives The Route – **Finance** a quantitative assessment, as to whether to accept or reject a loan and it can be used in conjunction with a qualitative judgment. It also provides a tool for evaluating a secured loan in comparison with past applications and any other investment.

The Route – **Finance** always asks that a Personal Guarantee be provided by the directors and/or shareholders of the company applying for the loan and the checklist records whether the borrower agrees to, or resists, that request. If the checklist records a 'resist', a reason needs to be provided. There may be an acceptable reason but, of course, The Route – **Finance** will seek to have as many layers of security and the largest amount of quality security as possible for each loan. This ensures that The Route – **Finance** Members' loans are as secure as possible.

There are other items in the checklist, such as:

In the security section:
- Is there to be a single or staged repayment of the loan?
- On what date is the loan to be repaid?
- Will there be a charge over the Intellectual Property (IP) of the business?
- Will there be a charge over the assets of the business?

In the identification section, the information requested invariably includes:
- The Certificates of Incorporation
- The Company number
- Its registered and trading addresses
- The number of directors
- The number of shareholders
- Any relevant insurance policies in force
- The CVs and biographies of the key staff
- The CVs of the shareholders and the directors
- Any other evidence that confirms that:
    - The borrower is an authorised trading company;
    - The company has been properly set up; and
    - It is a viable going concern.

In the financial section:
- The audited accounts

- Management accounts
- Balance sheet
- Profit and Loss statements
- A twelve-month cash flow forecast
- Any existing credit facilities the company may have in place
- Any outstanding debtors the company may have
- An investigation of any existing liabilities:
  — How old are they?
  — When do they fall due?
  — Are there any aggressive creditors?
  — Are there any debts due for imminent payment?
- Is any part of the loan going towards paying an existing liability?

All of the financial information is reviewed by a chartered accountant and his findings and comments are entered in the DD report.

Once all of these areas have been dealt with, The Route – **Finance** will start on the loan specifics and any related background for the DD. As each loan is different, there is not a set list of additional requirements. It depends on the loan itself. For example, with a property loan, you should always request a valuation of the property. You would also complete research on the geographical area in which the property is situated. You would wish to know the sales prices and valuations of similar properties in that area.

There will be other specific DD needs for a property. These could take the form of sales and marketing reports for the area, additional information provided by the borrower or third party information that builds a case to evidence whether this is a secure loan for The Route – **Finance** investors.

The Route – **Finance** will also verify the identity of any third parties involved in the transaction. The primary borrower may not be the only person involved in the deal. A third party is anyone else involved in the transaction. For example, the borrower may employ a management consultant, a valuer for the security, or the exit for the loan may be dependent on a third party providing funds.

The identities of any third parties are verified in order to confirm they do exist, and that they are credible and *bona fide*. Initially, The Route – **Finance** will perform a Companies House search to confirm the filing of company accounts is up-to-date, how long the company has been in existence, who the directors are, what other directorships the directors hold, and that there are no outstanding issues against the company or its directors. If there are any issues, they are investigated.

After all the different sections of the DD report have been completed a 'Notes' section is compiled, which is essentially a 'Copy and paste' of each question that has been asked of the borrower. This information is invariably in email format and is kept in folders in The Route – **Finance**'s back office systems. This is important because, even with all of the information a borrower can provide, there will invariably be additional questions.

Each question that arises during the DD is sent across to the borrower to be answered and is recorded in the 'Notes' section. Of course, every answer needs to be satisfactory. Unlike a bank loan application, this is not necessarily a lengthy review period. If an answer requires clarification or prompts further questions, The Route – **Finance** will email the borrower. If a satisfactory answer cannot be provided, the loan application will be rejected. Finally, once the DD report has been completed and the loan is deemed to have passed, it goes through the 'Sign off' stage.

In summary, the DD checklist document essentially provides all of the signatories a sound argument that as to why the secured loan in question is one that meets the criteria for 'secured loans at unsecured lending rates', particularly in terms of the security and the exit for repaying the loan.

If, for any reason, that is not the case, and any individual is not able to sign off the loan, they state the reasons why, and The Route – **Finance** will need to review the objection and either provide further information to clarify, or seek additional information from the borrower. Of course, although The Route – **Finance** tries to give each borrower the opportunity to prove a loan is worth financing, if the evidence collated cannot provide that reassurance, the loan application will be rejected.

Once 'Sign off' internally has occurred, the loan enters the 'Execution phase' of consulting with The Route – **Finance**'s legal partners to obtain their agreement and sign off. In addition to The Route – **Finance**'s in-house DD, there is a due diligence exercise undertaken by the lawyers. They provide a secondary layer of DD and have their own set of requirements that must be satisfied. Assuming this can also be achieved the secured loan can be presented to The Route – **Finance**'s PDP Member participants and the fund raise for the loan can be started.

CASE STUDY FOUR

The Opportunity
The Route – **Finance** was approached by a developer to provide finance to purchase commercial properties for onward sale to a leading supermarket chain . The loan was for £2.3 m over a 15 month term with a 3 month extension option.

The Security
The security for the loan was to be in three tiers and the aggregate of:
- A First Charge over a shopping centre valued at £2.3 m by a leading firm of surveyors;
- A First Charge over two other property assets valued at £2.2 m by the same surveyors;
- A First Charge over the borrowing company and its assets; and
- A negative pledge to be included in the legal documentation to ensure that no further debt can be raised against the three properties.

The Pricing
- The loan was to attract an interest premium for the PDP participants of 16 % per annum.

- In the event of non-repayment of the loan when it fell due, either in full or in part, a penalty premium of 2.5 % per month was to apply to the unpaid balance.

Repayment
- The loan is due to be repaid from the anticipated £5 m sale proceeds for the shopping centre.
- In addition, the shopping centre and the adjoining commercial site were due to generate an aggregate income of over £900,000 over the 15 month loan term.

Commentary

A shopping centre constructed in the 1990s with an area of 111,000 square feet and 553 parking spaces sits on a nine acre site. It is located close to a major UK city centre and its anchor tenant is a leading supermarket chain.

- In 2010 the supermarket entered into a joint venture to purchase the shopping centre and an adjoining site for £21.5 m.
- The deal was unable to conclude due the performance of the property market in that area of UK at that time. The vendor was not able to sell to the supermarket at a new, lower price with the amount of bank borrowing he had in place at the time.
- The Route – **Finance** was approached by a developer who has been offered a portfolio of discounted

properties, of which the shopping centre is one of the assets he has cherrypicked.
- The properties have been offered to the developer, unencumbered with debt.
- The developer intends to purchase the shopping centre and recommence negotiations with the supermarket.
- The owner of the shopping centre at the time of the 2010 negotiations has the existing and ongoing relationship with the supermarket and is to be paid a consultancy fee, to assist with the transaction, payable on completion of the sale.
- The developer will also purchase two further sites from the vendor that will form part of the security.
- The shopping centre and the adjoining commercial site are both income-producing assets, and are expected to generate income during the loan term of over £900,000.

The Key Risks
- The developer is unable to sell the shopping centre to the supermarket or any other potential buyer; and in addition
- The aggregate value of the shopping centre, the other two properties and the rent become worth less than the loan capital plus interest.

*How The Route – **Finance** Works for Small Businesses*

Assessment
- All properties were valued on a 'Red Book' basis, which is deemed suitable for lending purposes by RICS (Royal Institution of Chartered Surveyors), and backed by the surveyors' Professional Indemnity Insurance cover.
- The supermarket had already carried out the relevant retail reports and commissioned architect's drawings. It was due to receive board approval for the purchase in 2010, until the vendor pulled out.
- The current developer does not wish to sell the shopping centre for less than £4.5 m and expects the supermarket to pay in excess of £5 m.
- The developer is confident that the supermarket will proceed with the purchase of the site, as it was refused planning permission for three other sites in the area.
- Although the shopping centre has been valued at £2.3 m, the developer believes that the supermarket will place a value on owning the freehold to the site:
  — It will allow the supermarket to expand an existing store, to generate additional revenues, which is far cheaper than building a new one.
  — It protects the store by not allowing a competitor to buy the freehold for the site from which they operate.
- In the event that the supermarket does not wish to proceed with the purchase, the developer will seek to sell the site or the adjoining commercial site to another

supermarket chain or manage the assets itself to attract new tenants.
- The adjoining commercial site now has planning permission to convert it to retail which it did not have at the time of the 2010 deal.
- The developer will be contributing £1.2 m himself as part of the financing of the deal.
- The Route – **Finance** was satisfied by both the security and the repayment of the loan.

LOAN ACCEPTED
and presented to The Route – Finance's Platform Members*

*The loan has started and is due to be repaid in 2015.

CASE STUDY FIVE

The Opportunity
The Route – **Finance** was approached by a temporary structures company (TSC) based in London for finance to both repay money spent on a Management Buy Out (MBO) and provide working capital. The loan was for £1 m over a 12 month term with a three month extension option.

The Security
The security for the loan was a combination of a first charge over the company's shares and assets valued at £5.1 m, and the trademark, brand and IP valued at £360,000.

The Pricing
- The loan was to attract an interest premium for the PDP participants of 16 % per annum.
- In the event of non-repayment of the loan when it fell due, either in full or in part, a penalty premium of 3 % per month was to apply to the unpaid balance.

Repayment
- The unspent portion of the loan, after repayment of

£300,000 spent on the MBO, and the professional fees for arranging the loan.
- The anticipated sale of one or more of the temporary structures.
- In the event that the sale of a temporary structure did not complete within the loan term, the sale of other assets and/or trading revenues would provide the exit for the loan.
- The borrower anticipates that, from trading revenues alone, its 'cash at bank' figure prior to repayment of the loan would be over £2 m. This did not include the sale of any company assets.

Commentary
- A loan of £1 m was being sought as:
  — A working capital buffer; and
  — Repayment of the £300,000 spent on the MBO
- Whilst the MBO has already been paid for, the working capital had been used as a short-term solution and needed to be 'replaced' by new finance.
- TSC does not expect its cash balance to fall below £1.1 m during the term of the loan.
- The nature of TSC's project based business is 'spikey' in terms of revenues; therefore, a working capital buffer was required to support the cash flow if required.
- The assets have been independently valued, on a

replacement basis, at £5.1 m by a global build asset consultancy, in April 2013. This represents 510 % coverage of the loan capital.
- The Directors believe that at least £2.5 m could be achieved if the assets were to be sold on a '180 day' basis giving a minimum coverage of 250 % of the loan capital.

The Key Risks
- The borrower is unable to sell the main asset.
- The borrower is unable to sell sufficient other assets.
- The borrower is unable to generate sufficient revenues to repay the Loan, in tandem with the above sales and unspent cash.
- The value of the assets pledged as security falls below the loan capital plus interest amount.
- Trading revenues are not sufficient to allow the borrower to refrain from drawing down on the unspent balance of the Loan.

Assessment
- The borrower has forecasted total revenue of £9.2 m for the year, down from £18 m in 2012, which was the year that the summer Olympic Games was hosted in London.
- The borrower has confirmed orders for 37.5 % of their cash generation target for the year; the remainder is

dependent on converting pipeline business.
- The borrower has a £300,000 bank overdraft facility that was not being used at the time that the loan application was made to The Route – **Finance**.
- The two Directors have approximately £1.12 m invested personally in the business.
- The Route – **Finance** was satisfied with both the security and the repayment plan for the loan.

LOAN ACCEPTED
and presented to The Route – Finance's Platform Members*

*The loan was oversubscribed and the borrower applied for and was granted a second year loan in July 2014.

Bonus #2:

But how will it work for you and your personal circumstances? As an added bonus The Route – **Finance** is offering a fixed number of 'Be the Bank: How can using Secured Loans at unsecured lending rates work for you?' assessments. Simply go now to go to http://www.theroute-finance.com/be-the-bank and you will be able to obtain access to a complimentary assessment of your situation and suitability for using Secured Loans.

Chapter Three
WHY THE ROUTE – FINANCE WORKS FOR PARTICIPANTS

Now that The Route – **Finance** has found a suitable secured loan, assessed it through the DD process and qualified it, what happens next? It is presented to the PDP participants for their confirmed participation.

You might be asking, "Do all of these loans get fully funded?" The answer is "Yes". There is no shortage of demand from participants for secure loans at unsecured lending interest rates.

There is Always Demand for Secure Loans

As we discussed earlier the demand for secure, high return investments is of course high. And really, why would it not be? It is clearly an irresistible proposition.

In the 'Heads you win, tails you win' proposition of either:
- being repaid the loan capital via the exit borrower's exit strategy; or
- being repaid from the proceeds of selling the borrower's pledged assets

Investors find themselves in the much envied position of profiting without a significant risk of loss. For each secured loan, the PDP participants are informed of any risks as well as the loan terms.

Due to the stringent DD process undertaken by The Route – **Finance** and the strict vetting of any loans put before its PDP participants, The Route – **Finance** limits the risk to its investors as much as possible. As a result, The Route – **Finance** has built an enviable reputation, within its Membership and the broader business world, for presenting Secure High Return loans to PDP participants.

Becoming the Bank

Earlier it was discussed how difficult it is for SMEs to obtain the financing necessary to deliver the business plan and grow their businesses. There is an obvious, and significant, gap in the market that The Route – **Finance** is filling for these SMEs. Becoming the bank is almost a 'no-brainer', as the Americans might say, whilst this distortion between the high returns available and the low risk to capital exists.

Let us say that you are ready to take the step toward becoming a PDP participant. You have read about the process for selecting secured loans. However before we get into the wider discussion of the funding process and the life cycle of the loan, it makes sense to step back and discuss how one becomes a PDP participant in the first place. If you are interested in becoming a PDP Member and have picked up this book for that reason, you will probably want to know how to become a participant with access to The Route – **Finance**'s secured loans.

How to Become A Private Debt Platform (PDP) Participant

You may now feel that you are ready to become a PDP participant. However, you need to qualify by way of income or assets to do so. In order to become a PDP participant, you must meet the relevant criteria for this type of investment, namely, you must be certified as a 'High Net Worth individual' under the Financial Services and Markets Act 2000 (Financial Promotion) Order 2001.

To be certified, at least one of the following must apply:

a) You need to have an annual income of at least £100,000 during the financial year immediately preceding the date of your application;
AND/OR
b) You must have net assets of a minimum of £250,000, held throughout the financial year immediately preceding the

date of your application. Net assets for these purposes do not include:-

(i) A property that is your primary residence or any loan secured on that residence

(ii) Any rights under 'A qualifying contract of insurance' within the meaning of the Financial Services and Markets Act 2000 (Regulated Activities) Order 2001

OR

(iii) Any benefits, in the form of a pension or otherwise, which are payable on the termination of your employed service or on your death or retirement and to which you are, or your dependents are, or may be, entitled.

If you are qualified as a High Net Worth individual, you are welcome to apply to become a participant in The Route – **Finance**'s PDP.

*"Anyone involved in the area of management concerned with overseeing, designing, and controlling business operations will understand that their main responsibility is to ensure that those operations are efficient in terms of using as few resources as possible whilst still remaining effective in meeting the clients' requirements. The Route – **Finance**'s PDP lends itself perfectly to those objectives. A cleverly designed, process-driven product that can be replayed over and over again to deliver the kind of projects*

*Why The Route – **Finance** Works for Participants*

*that The Route – **Finance**'s Member clients desire, and in turn satisfying the business' need".*

— *Lisa McLeod*
Operations Director

How Does the PDP Work?

Once you have been pre-qualified as a High Net Worth investor, you mandate a sum of money to the PDP. That money is held within either a personal, or a Self Invested Personal Pension (SIPP), bank account to be used for participating in secured loans. (Please see the detailed information about Pension and SIPP accounts that follows.) Each participant is required to construct a 'Participation Mandate' specifying how they would like the money to be allocated and any restrictions. For example, not more than £50,000 per loan and no loans longer than eighteen months. The money is kept as cash in the bank account until a secured loan that meets the investment mandate is sourced and presented to you for confirmed participation, along with the other Members.

Once a secured loan is ready to be presented to PDP participants, a summary, called the 'Blueprint' sheet, is sent to all investors on the platform with a suggested participation amount based on their individual mandate. Participants, assuming they have no questions, can sign and return the email to confirm their participation. They also have the option to not participate, if they so choose.

Once the requisite confirmation emails have been received from the Members, and thus all the money to fund the loan has been raised, The Route – **Finance** will organise the preparation of the legal paperwork and instruct the formal completion. After the raise finance has been confirmed, participants will be:

- Emailed to explain the steps from confirmed participation to the loan starting;
- Provided with the formal loan paperwork; and
- Updated by email, normally every three months, during the loan term until the loan capital plus interest has been repaid. These updates invariably contain:
  — A narrative from the borrower as to the progress to exit and repayment;
  — Financial information, including a balance sheet, the 'Profit & Loss' statement and the cash flow actuals and forecast; and
  — Any relevant, ad hoc developments.
- The Route – **Finance** acts as Security Trustee, as explained earlier, to oversee and protect the PDP Members' interests, liaise with the borrower on the Members' behalf generally, and ensure adherence to the loan conditions as necessary.

- The Route – **Finance** will assist in liaising between the borrower and the lawyers when the borrower repays the loan capital and accrued interest.

The End of the Loan Term Outcomes

Although the normal and preferred outcome at the end of the loan term is for repayment of the loan capital and interest in full and on time, there are three possible scenarios that I shall explain below:

- Full repayment of the Loan capital plus interest on time: the borrower repays the loan in full along with all interest due on the loan end date.
- An agreed extension to the loan term for all or part of the Loan capital plus interest: the borrower, normally well before the loan end date, will seek agreement from the participants to an extension, normally short-term, for repayment of all or part of the money owed. This can either be completed:
  — Without a new loan term having to be set up with new legal paperwork. Normally the participants would agree to a short-term extension if it is no more than a few months and they would earn interest at the agreed penalty interest rate until the loan is repaid; or

- As a new loan with new terms that may include a revised interest rate or, term and/or security to satisfy the participants. This can be either the borrower or the PDP Members who wish to propose revised terms.
- Default leading to foreclosure and the sale of the assets pledged as security for the loan: Either at the end of the initial loan term or at the end of an agreed extension, if the borrower cannot repay the loan capital plus interest in full, the participants can choose to exercise their right to being repaid through the selling of the pledged assets. This is normally as the Members feel that either the borrower's exit plan is no longer credible or they feel it would be quicker to sell the assets than to agree to an extension. Normally, if the borrower still has a credible repayment plan, it is probably quicker to agree to an extension than to sell the assets through foreclosure.

However, it is the Member participants who decide this and not The Route – **Finance** or the borrower. Clearly as an extension must be agreed to, the borrower should, if at all possible, repay the loan in full, and on time, as he runs the risk, once the loan is in default, of foreclosure and the assets pledged as security being sold. The sale of assets as a result of foreclosure would normally, of course, realise a lower price than if sold under normal circumstances, but with the assets worth a minimum of

150 % of the loan capital plus interest there should normally always be sufficient money to repay the loan capital plus interest in full. The participants can only receive back what they are due (capital, interest and any penalty interest levied). Any surplus is returned to the borrower after payment of all professional fees incurred during the process of foreclosing on the loan and selling the assets.

PENSIONS AND SELF INVESTED PERSONAL PENSION (SIPP) ACCOUNTS

"Equity-level returns with a corporate bond level of risk (or arguably even lower) – a very attractive proposition for any investor. The targeted 15%p.a. if compounded in a tax efficient environment could exponentially increase investors' assets, from £250k to over £1m, in just ten years. In my view, everyone of the correct profile should consider exposing at least a part of their pension fund to this asset class, whilst this distortion exists."

— Harnesh Fhalora DipPFS
Head of The Route – ***Future***

*Where the term 'SIPP' has been used you may also relate the text to Small Self Administered Schemes (SSAS), which have similar rules.

Managing your own pension investments is not appropriate for everyone – you need to be satisfied that you have:

- The necessary skills and experience to make the key decisions required to enable you to meet your objectives and plans for retirement; and
- The time necessary to apply this knowledge consistently and regularly, over the years until retirement or drawing on pension benefits.

Pensions and Self Invested Personal Pension (SIPP) Accounts

Pensions are long-term saving vehicles that carry significant tax advantages. No withdrawals from a pension are permitted, before the age of 55 and there are restrictions around the income that can be taken.

*The value of the favourable tax treatment will depend on your individual circumstances. Please note that The Route – **Finance** does not provide tax advice. In addition, you should be aware that tax and/or pension rules may change in the future.*

Just as is the case with traditional pension funds, the value of SIPP investments can fall as well as rise.

*The Route – **Finance** always recommends that you to obtain Independent Financial Advice throughout the term of the pension contract.*

What Is A Pension?

A pension is a long-term investment that aims to build up a fund for your retirement in a tax efficient way. The value of your pension will depend on a number of factors, including when you start saving, how long you save for, how much you save and in what assets your money is invested. The money you save within a pension is invested, and when you retire, or reach a certain age (normally from age 55 at the earliest), you have flexible access to the fund, 25% of which can be as a tax-free lump sum.

Let us take a look at the table below, which shows how a few small changes* could substantially increase your fund at retirement age, based on a starting fund of £100,000:

	10 years	20 years	30 years
@ 5% p.a. growth	£162,889	£265,329	£432,194
@ 10% p.a. growth	£259,374	£672,749	£1,744,940
@ 15% p.a. growth	£404,555	£1,636,653	£6,621,177

*The investment term in years versus the percentage growth annually.

To put this into context, the FTSE 100 grew on average by 7.72 % annually between the years 1993 and 2013 inclusive (Source: Trustnet).

There are various types of pensions available. Traditional pension plans often have limited investment choice i.e. only allowing you to invest in the range of funds from a single life assurance company, and therefore only covering a relatively small number of investment possibilities. A SIPP offers the greatest choice with access to a much wider range of investment options whilst maintaining all of the tax advantages of traditional pensions. The only restrictions being the relevant HMRC rules and what the SIPP provider chooses to include in

Pensions and Self Invested Personal Pension (SIPP) Accounts

its offering, although most SIPPs allow a 'whole of market' choice of available investment funds.

In terms of choice, SIPPs can provide access to a broad range of funds allowing you to invest in the best performing funds in the market and the flexibility to combine these with direct share holdings, Exchange Traded Funds (ETFs), government and corporate bonds, and importantly for this discussion, The Route – **Finance**'s PDP secured loans.

If you already have a company pension scheme, you can still open a SIPP and contribute to it, subject to overall limits on contributions. Thus, a SIPP need not take the place of your existing pension provision, but can supplement it. For example, if you are concerned that the fund that you are building up in your company pension scheme will not be enough, you can use a SIPP to top it up.

You are allowed to contribute to multiple pension schemes within the same tax year as long as your combined pension contributions do not exceed certain annual limits. As well as receiving new contributions, you can also transfer funds, either personal or company, already accumulated in other pension plans into your SIPP to benefit from the wider investment choice and added flexibility that a SIPP can offer. If you choose to transfer other schemes into your SIPP, you need to ensure that you are not giving up valuable benefits in the current pension arrangements. Bringing all of your pensions together within a SIPP should make your retirement savings easier to manage and can significantly reduce the associated paperwork. You should always seek Independent Financial Advice if you wish to assess whether it is better to retain your old pension arrangements or consolidate them into fewer schemes.

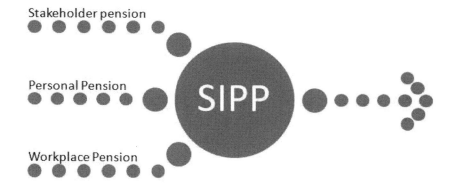

Who Can Have A SIPP?

Any UK resident (or individual with earnings chargeable to UK income tax) under the age of 75 years of age may open a SIPP, including Crown employees. In addition, non-UK residents may have a SIPP and continue to invest the money therein whilst they are abroad.

Pensions and Self Invested Personal Pension (SIPP) Accounts

The Tax Advantages

As SIPPs are subject to the same access restrictions as other pensions, for many investors, the attractive tax benefits, wide range of investments and control that SIPPs offer outweigh these perceived constraints.

As a pension, a SIPP has three significant tax advantages. Please note that tax rules can change, and the value of the tax relief will depend on your individual circumstances, but over time, these tax benefits should significantly increase the value of your retirement savings:

- **Tax relief on the contributions:** the payments that you make to your SIPP will attract generous income tax relief at your highest marginal rate- to a maximum of 45 % currently.

- **Tax efficient returns:** Any profits you make on the investments inside a SIPP are free from income and capital gains taxes.

- **Tax-free withdrawals:** From April 2015, once you reach 55 years of age you may withdraw the fund either as a single lump sum or a series of lump sums over time – 25% of any such lump sum always being paid to you free from tax.

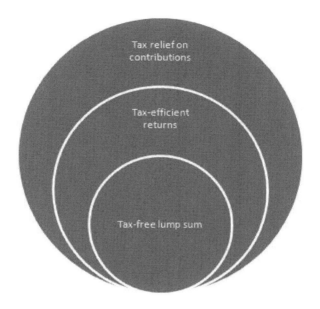

What Are The Restrictions?

You can make unlimited contributions to a pension but there are restrictions to the amount of you can obtain tax relief on. Whilst funds invested in a SIPP are usually not subject to income or capital gains tax, there could be tax charges if your savings within a SIPP exceed certain 'Annual' and/or 'Lifetime' limits.

An increasing number of investors are choosing to access The Route – **Finance**'s secured loans through their SIPPs, given the benefits outlined earlier. A SIPP may not be the correct choice

Pensions and Self Invested Personal Pension (SIPP) Accounts

for everyone, so it is important to take Independent Financial Advice. The Route – **Finance** does not provide this advice but can introduce you to an Independent Financial Adviser to talk you through your options and to assess if this is the best solution in relation to your overall financial planning.

You can find out how by going to the website www.theroute-finance.com.

Bonus #3:

The preceding information provides an enlightening overview of how you can utilise your pension, in the form of a SIPP or SASS, to take advantage of mandating money to Secured Loans. You should always obtain independent financial avice if you are considering the transfer of one or more of your pensions. For a valuable insight into the key aspects you should consider, go to http://www.theroute-finance.com/be-the-bank to download for free *'Your guide to pension transfers.'* This guide explains, in simple terms, **what you really need to know.**

CASE STUDY SIX

*"There is an innate appeal to The Route – **Finance**'s PDP: business owners need access to lenders who are prepared to understand their business's needs, and Members welcome good quality loans offering attractive returns. The right secured loan will always therefore be of interest to The Route – **Finance**, and we will work hard to assess it so that Members can lend with confidence. Get the formula right and not only do investors enjoy good financial returns, but there is satisfaction in seeing another UK business grow and achieve its objectives along the way."*

— Simon Pimblett
Head of Research & Development

The Opportunity

The Route – **Finance** was approached by a residential property company, wishing to raise finance for the development of part of the site of a closed hospital in Southern England. The loan was for £1.5 m over a term of twelve months with a three-month extension option.

The Security

The security for the loan was to be in four tiers and the aggregate of:

Pensions and Self Invested Personal Pension (SIPP) Accounts

- A First Charge against the building being developed (Court 1) valued at £2.65 m:
- A First Charge against the borrower company's assets held including a second charge against the entire property development valued at £1.03 m;
- A Personal Guarantee provided by the developer for 25 % of any outstanding capital plus interest; and
- A Negative Pledge included in the legal documentation in order that no further debt could secured on Court 1.

In addition, the loan was to be drawn down in phases, as per the cash flow provided by the developer and agreed with the building contractor. Each drawdown was to be authorised by The Route – **Finance** upon receiving a report from the administering architects, confirming that the work had been completed to the required standard.

The Pricing
- The loan was to attract an interest premium for the PDP participants of 16 % per annum.
- In the event of non-repayment of the loan when it fell due, either in full or in part, a penalty premium of 3 % per month was to apply to the unpaid balance.

Repayment
1. The proceeds of the sale of the 67 units in Court 1 were anticipated to gross £8.89 m, made up of:

- 31 units already at Exchange stage, having paid 10% non-refundable deposits These were expected to raise a total of £2.7 m (£3 m less the 10 % deposit already paid).
- The remaining 36 units which were expected to be sold within the loan term. The average sale price of the remaining unsold Prime sea view units was £148,700 giving an aggregate value of £5.35 m. The sales of these units had been held back to secure the highest possible prices.

Commentary
- There was a total loan requirement of £2 m to complete the internal units for sale.
- The hospital closed in the mid 1990s.
- After several years of dereliction and vandalism the site was purchased by a property developer in 2004 and planning permission was granted for the conversion of the buildings to 272 apartments. Construction commenced in 2006.
- The project was financed by a major bank that collapsed in September 2008. This left the project without funding and has forced the development into the hands of the receivers who were instructed by the bank's administrators to sell the assets.

*Why The Route – **Finance** Works for Participants*

- Court 1 is a new stand-alone building within the site that is to comprise 67 apartments with underground parking. There were to be 12 three-bed and 55 two-bed apartments, providing a total saleable area of 49,500 square feet.
- The developer had already spent approximately £1 m on court 1 in order to complete the external frame of the building.
- The loan of £1.5 m was applied for to finance building the internal units in Court 1.
- A second loan of £500,000 has already been obtained from another source. This has a second charge, in terms of security, *behind* The Route – **Finance** investors.
- The two loans would provide sufficient funding to complete all 67 units of Court 1 within ten months.

The Key Risks
- The exchanged sales on Court 1 do not complete.
- Insufficient further sales of Court 1 units materialise.
- The aggregate value of Court 1 and the second charge against the site together fall below the level of the loan capital plus interest.

Assessment
- The 31 exchanged sales had already paid a non-refundable deposit of 10 % of the purchase price.

- Further pre-sales of the units had been delayed until after the finance for the completion of the development had been secured.
- These exchanged sales were due to complete and the 90 % balance paid seven days after the units had been finished.
- The units have been marketed using a low-key advertising campaign. A larger promotional campaign was to commence once the additional finance had been confirmed.
- The PDP loan money was to be held in an escrow bank account and only drawn down in accordance with the build contractor's fixed fee contract, and the necessary 'Application for payments for work' forms completed.
- The architects were to provide a report to ensure the full value of the work has been completed in accordance with the fixed fee contract, and to the required standard.
- All 67 units were scheduled to be finished by the end of month nine of the twelve-month loan, as per the fixed fee build contract.
- The Route – **Finance** was satisfied with both the security and the repayment for the loan.

*Why The Route – **Finance** Works for Participants*

THE LOAN WAS ACCEPTED*
and presented to The Route – Finance's Platform Members

*The loan was oversubscribed and the three-month extension option was taken up. The loan was repaid in full in August 2014 repaying an interest of 25.33% over the seventeen month term.

Chapter Four
COMMONLY ASKED QUESTIONS AND ANSWERS

Question: What is the vetting process like?

Once received, a loan application must fit within the mandate criteria for a PDP secured loan, otherwise it will be turned down. The key criteria are as follows:

Loan amount: £1 m to £2.5 m. Although larger loans may be considered.
Short-term: Less than 24 months, but typically no longer than 18 months.
Fully secured: By way of saleable, realisable assets that provide at least 150 % coverage for the loan capital plus interest.
Loan interest: Targeting 15 % per annum.
Exit strategy: Includes a capital event that is likely and probable.
Penalty premium: A minimum of 150 % of the loan interest, pro rata.

Generally, introducers will pre-vet projects, as they are familiar with The Route – **Finance**'s PDP model and would not want to waste our or their time. A borrower who contacts The Route –

*Why The Route – **Finance** Works for Participants*

Finance directly may not be familiar with the PDP requirement and, therefore, a discussion regarding the criteria and the type of financing The Route – **Finance** offers is normally held. If the company in question has assets and is seeking a loan that matches the above criteria, The Route – **Finance** may be able to assist. A little more work is usually required, but The Route – **Finance** is happy to engage with business owners to discuss their funding requirements.

From a borrower/introducer perspective, the initial assessment is very prompt. Assuming the above points are provided clearly, The Route – **Finance** aims to make an initial assessment decision within 48 hours, as it will be immediately clear to the team if it is a loan that The Route – **Finance** can consider and is likely to accept, subject to satisfactory DD. If a loan is rejected, the borrower and the introducer will be informed as to the reason(s) why and, if possible, what the borrower would need to do to make it an acceptable proposal. If the proposal is acceptable, subject to satisfactory DD, the borrower and introducer are informed accordingly and the DD phase can commence.

The next stage is the DD process. This takes a forensic approach. A list of the information needed is provided to the borrower requesting items such as the balance sheet, Profit and Loss statement, cash flow forecasts, the valuations of the assets and the accountant's details. Once answers from the borrower have been received, questions invariably follow where clarification or expansion is needed. This part of the process is more formal than the initial stage, and the items requested must be provided. If not initially satisfactory a suitable, acceptable explanation must be given. The financial information is reviewed by The Route – **Finance**'s chartered accountant as well as the other members of The Route – **Finance**'s investment committee who may be asked to provide an opinion as required.

The internal DD report is then completed; it has three key components — information, evidence and questions. Much of the information and the supporting evidence will have already been provided by the borrower. In addition, The Route – **Finance** will conduct its own research to ensure that any information provided by the borrower is accurate. The Route – **Finance** will build a file of information to reach a standard that will allow it to make a decision and recommend to the investment committee for 'sign off', if appropriate.

Once The Route – **Finance** agrees internally that an acceptable quality standard has been reached, the report will be circulated to the investment committee for review and 'signed off', if each member of the committee agrees that the loan is suitable for distribution to the PDP participants. Agreement from each member of the committee is required before acceptance. If a project fails to satisfy any member the project will revert to The

Route – **Finance**'s assessor working on the loan and, if necessary, the borrower to address the concern or answer the question. If the investment committee member cannot be satisfied, the loan application project will fail DD. The borrower is informed, provided with the reason(s) why and what could be done to rectify the failure.

Question: Are all loan applications approved? Why might they not be approved?

Only the loan applications that are approved are selected for distribution to The Route – **Finance**'s PDP participants. A borrower's application will be declined for a variety of different reasons. Here are some of the situations where loans were not approved and the reasons why:

A Distressed Renewable Electricity Plant
- All the project terms were within the remit with sufficient security, probable exit and acceptable premium.
- The security was the renewable electricity generation equipment and the company's leased commercial property.
- One of the individuals, involved in an advisory role to the borrower, had recently been 'Struck off' by the SRA (Solicitors Regulation Authority) for gross negligence

and money laundering. This information had not been provided during the initial loan assessment, as the borrower had not been made aware of it.
- The individual's wife was also a 50 % shareholder in the holding company of the borrower.
- The Route – **Finance** was not comfortable with the involvement of this individual or the suggestions from the borrower as to how they felt they could rectify this. The loan application was declined.

Solar Farm
- The company was seeking a loan to purchase the leases to plots of land across UK.
- The security offered was the leased land.
- Once the leases had been granted, the lender could apply for planning permission to install solar farms on the sites.
- The sites' leases were of negligible value, if the permissions were not granted. The loan application was declined.

A Web Based Publication
- The owner of the website was seeking to expand his business.
- The website makes money from sales of literature.
- The literature was offered as security for the loan but

Commonly Asked Questions and Answers

after a discussion it was clear the borrower needed equity and not debt finance.
- The loan application was declined.

A Cut Flower Provider
- The Company is a major cut flower producer in the UK.
- The security offered for the loan was its physical stock, specifically plant bulbs.
- The stock required tightly controlled storage conditions to ensure it did not perish.
- The Route – **Finance** took the view that the stock would be difficult to realise. The loan application was declined.

A 'TV App' Company
- The 'App' company was seeking to expand its business into gambling and further advertising.
- The security offered was computer hardware and a long-term lease for a data centre, which was a former MI5 communications facility.
- The company was unwilling to pay The Route – **Finance** a DD fee. The loan application did not proceed beyond the initial assessment stage and was declined.

A Mongolian Fluorite Mine
- The borrower was seeking £1 m to commence extraction of fluorite from a mine in Mongolia.
- The security was the mine itself.

- The geographical location of the asset was the main concern and no valuation had been provided. The loan application was declined.

An Entertainment Company
- A short-term loan for working capital was applied for prior to a foreign investor providing equity capital.
- The security was an entertainment product that could not be produced on a mass scale and did not have many orders due to its high price.
- The company was in its early growth stage and the security and exit were not within the criteria specified. The application for a loan was declined.

An African Security Company
- A short-term loan was required for a company that provides security for an oil and gas exploration company in the Horn of Africa.
- The security was the assets purchased with the loan plus a Kenyan residential property.
- The exploration company was due to offer a lucrative contract to the borrower.
- The geographical location of the assets in Somaliland and Kenya and the business plan risk were not acceptable. The loan application was declined.

An American State Film Tax Credits Proposition
- A loan was required to cash flow the State's film tax credits.
- The tax credits were to be the main security.
- The borrower company's directors were unwilling to offer personal guarantees as additional security.
- The loan application was declined.

Question: Within the process, how are gains distributed to the Platform participants? Are they easily able to withdraw money from the Platform or is tied up for a long period of time?

Once Platform Members have decided to participate in a project, they do not have access to their capital during the term of the loan. When a loan has completed the capital and interest are transferred to your personal, trust or SIPP bank account, either directly from the borrower or via the solicitors dealing with the loan.

The Route – **Finance** asks that investors pledge funds to the platform for a minimum of three years. This though is a 'Gentleman's Agreement' and money can be withdrawn earlier, if required, when it is not lent to a borrower in a secured loan. This Gentleman's Agreement term is necessary as it is difficult to match loans to pledged funds if investors remove funds from the platform at short notice. Of course, assuming the investor gives The Route – **Finance** sufficient notice of withdrawal, The Route – **Finance** can plan ahead adequately with matching secured loans to mandated money.

Question: How are Platform participants updated on their loan investments?

- Initial Loan Confirmation: At the start of each loan a document dealing with the transaction and confirming the secured loan's details will be provided by the lawyers. Standard practice is for the originals to be held within the lawyers' strong room, with scanned copies sent to participants. Originals are, of course, available to be viewed on request.

- Quarterly Reports: The platform participants are sent reports by The Route – **Finance** normally every three months for each Secured loan they are participating in. These reports contain a narrative with respect to repayment of the loan, the related financial information of Profit & Loss, balance sheet and cash flow forecasts and details of any ad hoc developments. Although the information is provided by the borrower, The Route – **Finance** always:
  — Reviews and clarifies any misleading information or asks for additional text to be added if necessary; and

— Provides a summary of the key points to be sent with the information provided by the borrower.

- End of Loan statement: Upon repayment of a loan each participant will receive a statement of lending, confirming the amount provided, the repayment date for the loan and the amount capital and interest paid.

Annual Reviews: Investors are also entitled to an annual review meeting as part of their Route – **Finance** Membership. At that meeting, a review of the 'market space' and each of the participants' loans will be provided.

Question: Can investors and borrowers come from anywhere in the world?

Yes, they can be based anywhere, although they tend to either be:
- UK resident; or
- Have significant UK sited assets within or outside of a pension.

CASE STUDY SEVEN

The Opportunity
The Route – **Finance** was approached by a waste management company in the North of England, WasteCo. The borrower wished to raise £2 m over a term of twelve months with a three-month extension option.

The Security
The security for the loan was to be a combination of a First Charge against commercial land valued at £5.25 m, a first charge 'All monies' debenture over WasteCo and a negative pledge so that no additional debt could be secured against the assets pledged as security.

The Pricing
- The loan would attract an interest premium for the PDP participants of 16 % per annum.
- In the event of non-repayment of the loan in full when it fell due, a penalty rate of 3 % per month would apply.

Repayment
- The loan was to be repaid via the raising of £70 m of

Commonly Asked Questions and Answers

project finance from a number of different debt and equity sources.

Commentary
- WasteCo was established in 2011 after several years of 'Proof of concept' work by the founder investors and shareholders.
- WasteCo secured an option to purchase a site in the North of England, with planning permission to build an EfW power generation plant.
- WasteCo signed a Pre-Engineering Procurement & Construction (EPC) contract with a multinational company that was to design and build the power plant.
- Once the land was purchased, it was expected that the full EPC would be granted. This would result in the value of the land increasing to £5.25 m and allow further equity to be raised.
- WasteCo was seeking to raise £2 m in total as a secured loan to fund:
  - The acquisition of the land; and
  - Working capital.
- It was proposed that £1 m of the loan would be released initially to purchase the land valued at £2 m. The balance of the purchase would be paid for by WasteCo.
- Once the EPC had been granted the value of the land would increase to £5.25 m, as per a surveyor's report,

backed by their Professional Indemnity Insurance cover.
- The second £1 m of loan was planned to be released as the asset value would have increased to £5.25 m.
- If the EPC had not been granted, the remaining loan would not be released to the borrower, as the security would not be sufficient. However, interest would continue to accrue on the entire amount of the loan whether drawn or undrawn.

The Key Risks:
- No debt or equity is raised; and
- The value of the commercial land falls.

Assessment
- The Professional Indemnity cover benefit of the valuation was to be assigned to the PDP lenders.
- A full EPC was unable to be granted until the land was owned by WasteCo and an initial payment made to the company that was to design and build the power plant.
- Once the EPC was in place, the value of the land increases as the land with planning permission, plus EPC can be sold as a package to an incoming party for development.
- The multinational company that was due to design and build the power plant was supported by a government backed financier, who was due to provide £26 m of debt funding.

- WasteCo had spent circa £1 m to date to reach this stage.
- The Route – **Finance** was satisfied with both the security and the repayment of the loan.

THE LOAN WAS ACCEPTED
and presented to The Route – Finance's
Platform Members*

*The loan was oversubscribed but did not start as the borrower elected to obtain the debt finance from its equity provider.

Chapter Five:
WHY USE THE ROUTE – FINANCE?

After all that has been discussed in this book, it may seem odd to be asking this question. However, the question does bear asking, especially as we are talking about investing your money. Why invest your money in secured loans sourced by The Route – **Finance**? In the earlier text I have discussed how The Route – **Finance** operates in sourcing and assessing secured Loans and how it acts as the Security Trustee during the life of the loans. This level of scrutiny and detail is invariably not provided by others offering debt finance investment opportunities. Other companies' processes are not as thorough, or as transparent, in ensuring that the risk to their clients is both as low as possible and fully understood. In summary, there has been put in place a comprehensive process and way of doing things that other companies simply do not emulate. The Route – **Finance** thoroughness underpins the PDP. Our integrity and reputation are of paramount importance.

> "Speaking directly to SME owners, it is apparent that the loans offered by The Route – **Finance** are meeting a crucial finance demand. Whilst addressing the lack of SME lending, the feedback

I also receive is that the simplicity and speed of the application process is far more straightforward than dealing with a mainstream bank.

*Business owners I meet are frustrated and have trust issues with these banks. They are unable to obtain the credit facilities they need without going through a seemingly never-ending application process that invariably ends in a refusal. The facilities offered by The Route – **Finance** provide the certainty of funding that SME company owners require in order that they can focus on building their businesses".*
— Iain Burke, Head of The Route – **Finance**'s Technical Team

The Route – Finance's Ten Defining Differences for Secured Loans on the PDP

The Key Things That Separate The Route – Finance From The Rest:

1. Interest premiums earned by participants are generally higher at a targeted 15 % per annum where almost all other secured lending is in single figures.
2. The Route – **Finance** is more experienced, having been in business longer than most, if not all, of its competition.
3. The Route – **Finance** only deals in secured lending and does not offer a mix of secured and unsecured loans.
4. The terms of The Route – **Finance**'s secured loans are

generally shorter, at 12 to 15 months whilst other companies' loans are longer, often as long as five years.
5. A higher minimum participation per secured loan of £25,000, i.e. the platform is specifically for 'High net worth' investors.
6. Participants can participate via cash, trust funds, and/or pension monies via a SIPP. They can also mandate company deposits.
7. The assessing and underwriting process is more thorough and therefore normally longer.
8. Platform participants pay an annual The Route – **Finance** Membership fee of £300 and have access to a dedicated Relationship Manager and contractual service features.
9. Participants have structured review meetings on both their current secured loans and the market sector for debt finance.
10. Participants have access to complementary services via The Route – **City Wealth Club**'s Membership proposition (see Appendix).

The Route – **Finance** strives each day to provide the optimal borrowing and lending platform for its clients. I invite you to learn more about The Route – **Finance**'s way of doing things at www.theroute-finance.com.

An Encouraging Postscript

In March 2014, the UK.gov website requested consultation on whether the government should legislate to help match SMEs that have been rejected for loans with challenger banks and alternative finance providers who are looking to offer funding. The consultation also asked questions about the mechanics of delivering such a measure if the government decided to so legislate, and set out the government's preferred approach of requiring banks to refer details of SMEs, that have been rejected for loans, to a platform or platforms so that they can be accessed by challenger banks and other providers of finance. Among the facts cited in this consultation request are:

- Challenger banks are new banks to the UK lending sector.
- At present, the largest four banks account for over 80 % of UK SMEs' main banking relationships.
- In the recent Department of Business, Innovation and Skills (BIS)/BMG Research study which estimated that the majority (71 %) of businesses who seek funding only approach one provider. The study also noted that in more than half of all cases, the provider the SME approaches will be their main bank.
- The BIS/BMG Research study found that 37 % of businesses appear to give up their search for finance and cancel their spending plans after their first rejection.

- The BIS/BMG Research study found that only 6 % of SMEs declined for loans are referred to alternative funding by their bank, and just a further 11 % are offered alternative funding or advice.

The government announced at Autumn Statement 2013 that it would consult on proposals to require banks to share information on their SME customers with other lenders through Credit Reference Agencies (CRA). The government launched this consultation on 26th December 2013 and intends to legislate as soon as parliamentary time allows. The proposals are intended to improve the ability of challenger banks and alternative finance providers to conduct accurate SME credit scoring and, by levelling the playing field between providers, make it easier for SMEs to seek a loan from a lender other than their bank. A better understanding of the SME sector should also stimulate competition and innovation in SME lending, improving the cost and quality of services offered.

More recently, speaking at the FSB 40th anniversary conference, the Chancellor of the Exchequer, George Osborne, announced how proposals published on 28th March 2014 aim to make it easier for SMEs to find alternative loan providers. The consultation referred to asked whether the government should legislate to require lenders to release information on SMEs they reject for finance, so that those SMEs can be identified and approached by alternate credit providers. The Chancellor also said:

> "The success of small and medium-sized business is key to the government's long-term economic plan. That's why we are fully focused on making sure businesses can get the finance they need to grow and create jobs. This includes actively supporting innovative new forms of business lending.
>
> We're setting out new proposals that will help match up other lenders with small businesses that may have been turned down for a loan by a large bank. A big bank saying 'no' should not be the end of the line for a small business. Now, with our plan, it won't be".

The ultimate aim is for new online platforms to be created so that lenders can find SMEs that are looking for a loan, but have been rejected first time around. (Big banks account for the vast majority of main SME banking relationships [over 80 %], but innovative new forms of credit, such as peer-to-peer lending and crowd-funding platforms, are being created in the UK all the time.)

The proposals will bridge the gap between SMEs not knowing other lending options could meet their needs, and alternative lenders not knowing these businesses need a loan.

Additionally, as Business Secretary Vince Cable said:

"Too many businesses are put off looking for finance if they are turned down by their bank. By putting the onus on banks to refer these businesses to other sources of finance, we can help make sure the potential of the country's small businesses isn't lost. A better referrals system will be good for competition and good for the economy".

In addition in December 2013 a report was produced: THE RISE OF FUTURE FINANCE-The UK Alternative Finance Benchmarking Report which was a joint project written by:

Liam Collins, Nesta
Richard Swart, University of California, Berkeley
Bryan Zhang, University of Cambridge

Key Findings:
- The UK alternative finance market grew by 91 % from £492 m in 2012 to £939 m in 2013.
- This headline figure hides a diverse market that covers many different activities serving a variety of funding needs.
- The UK alternative finance market provided £463 m worth of early-stage, growth and working capital to over 5,000 start-ups and SMEs in the UK from 2011-13, of which £332 m was accumulated in 2013 alone.

An Encouraging Postscript

- We can cautiously predict that the UK alternative finance market will grow to £1.6 bn in 2015 and provide £840 m worth of business finance for start-ups and SMEs in 2014.

Alternative finance intermediaries have been growing in size and impact in recent years in the UK as they attempt to provide much needed capital to individuals and businesses. This report presents the results from the first survey of the UK's alternative finance sector. The research presents the size and growth of alternative finance activities such as crowdfunding and peer-to-peer lending in terms of amounts raised, ventures funded and individuals contributing funds.

> **Bonus #4:**
>
> To bring it all together and see it work for you. The Route – **Finance** is offering a free year's complimentary Route – **Finance** Membership to the first 50 readers* who respond by going to *http://www.theroute-finance.com/be-the-bank* and applying successfully. The Membership will provide access to all the services currently provided to Members, which will be described in more detail on the website.
>
> * Offer is restricted to readers who are not at present Members of The Route – **City wealth club** or any of its subsidiaries or The Route – **Finance**.

APPENDIX

The Route – Finance & The Route – City wealth club Membership: Cost and Services

	The Route – City wealth club	The Route – Finance
Cost	£1 or 2k per annum	£300 per annum
The services of:		
A Relationship Manager	√	√
Advice on / Introduction to:		
Investment, estate planning, retirement and insurance solutions	√	
Property lending advice, Stamp duty & property investment opportunities	√	
Sophisticated planning for all personal taxes	√	
Syndicated investment opportunities	√	√
Meetings:		
Annual Review (APFR)	√	
Investment Review (ISR)	√	
Mortgage, Stamp Duty & Property Investment Review meeting	√	
Tax Planning Review	√	
Private Debt Platform & Equity Investment Ventures Review Meeting	√	√
Other:		
Project updates	√	√
Market Commentary e.g. Budget report	√	√

Testimonials for
The Route — Finance

"I am happy to invest in these projects as they provide a relatively secure investment with significant returns – something that has been missing from the market for some time. The process runs smoothly and the nature of the investments means that they are easy to understand and to get confidence in."

— Neil Jackson, Winchester, Hampshire UK; ex Head of European Power, Barclays Capital.

"In general, I feel that there is a best effort to present the best investment opportunities, so The Route — **Finance** is targeting the long-term relationship rather than maximising fees. In addition to the aligned interests, there is proper expertise to effectively identify those best cases and discount the average/subpar ones. Overall, a very solid platform."

The proof is in the pudding - the investments are working out, market and enterprise risk is not eliminated but are minimised and it seems the approved projects are the ones with the best risk-return profiles. ... Overall, very professional and thorough."

— Atanas Krastanoff; London, UK; Director of Precious Metals Trading, Citigroup

"The Route — **Finance's** due diligence process was well organised, straight-forward and pragmatic. Whilst there was the proper level of probing, it was generally stress-free.

The Route — **Finance** facility was ideal in filling a gap left by bank lenders for our type of asset finance. And, they were much more straight forward in negotiation than the conventional asset based lenders."

> **—John Harriss, Director, RJH (MARGATE) ONE LTD, Shipley, UK**

"The Route — **Finance** was a vital source of working capital at a critical stage of my business' development. When other finance options were not credible or of the right scale, The Route — **Finance** was able to take the time to review and assess the business case, and then tailor a package of funding that met the needs of the project.

The Route — **Finance** was professional and transparent throughout, and worked rapidly to form its experienced assessment. Once the required preparations had been made, The Route — **Finance** was able to seamlessly present the package for consideration by its funding base, respond to investor queries and marshal the required grouping of investors to best match the funding proposal. Following a successful fundraise, The

Testimonials

Route — **Finance** implemented a monitoring regime that had a light touch, but was thorough and comprehensive, for the interest of all parties. Further, The Route was always on hand to address queries during the lifetime of the agreement, and proactively support a flexible range of funding approaches to address a dynamic and evolving Company business plan. ... Without hesitation I would work with The Route — **Finance** again and would recommend its service to organisations in need of a responsive, nimble and professional funding partner."

— **Richard Van den Berg, Director, Coastal Marine Renewables Limited, London, UK.**

"Since the late 2000's financial crisis, and as a medium sized developer, we have found that there has had to be a move towards private and alternative methods of financing property development, particularly as the mainstream lenders have exited the market on mass.

We were introduced to The Route — **Finance** by a third party broker that we have worked with previously, and we are extremely grateful that he has brokered a relationship that we see as being on going for many years to come.

Our main point of contact at The Route — **Finance** has been the same from introduction to loan completion. We have found this to be extremely helpful in creating a strong and positive working relationship and have found the organisational ability of The Route — **Finance** to be exceptional in understanding a complex development project. We see The Route — **Finance** more as a partner in the relationship rather than pure lender. We will continue to build an ongoing relationship with The Route — **Finance** for this project and beyond and for other exciting projects that we are currently considering.

We would have no hesitation in recommending any prospective borrower to The Route – **Finance**, with the confidence that if there is a viable development project presented, then Route will provide its full commitment to it."

— **Howard Tolman, Director and Shareholder of Beta Gamma, London, UK.**

Printed in Great Britain
by Amazon.co.uk, Ltd.,
Marston Gate.